EMILY BRONTË REAPPRAISED

A VIEW FROM THE TWENTY-FIRST CENTURY

CLAIRE O'CALLAGHAN

Saraband

Published by Saraband
Digital World Centre
1 Lowry Plaza, The Quays
Salford M50 3UB
www.saraband.net

ISBN: 9781912235056
ebook: 9781912235230

Printed and bound in Great Britain by Clays Ltd, St Ives plc.

10 9 8 7 6 5 4 3 2 1

TITLE PAGE: *The 19th-century 'Humbert' portrait. Depictions of Emily,
including those that are disputed, are discussed on pages 164–66.*

CONTENTS

INTRODUCTION   1

ONE: THE LIFE AND WORKS OF EMILY   13
   The Early Years 14; Toy Soldiers 22;
   Diary Papers 24; Growing Pains 27; Final Days 31;
   Chronology of Emily's Life & Works 35

TWO: EMILY – THE BIOGRAPHERS' TALES   39
   Through Charlotte's Eyes, Darkly 41; To Be Forever
   Unstable 49; Emily: Friend, Friendly or Foe? 59

THREE: ELLIS BELL   63
   Emily's 'Rhymes' 65; Gondal 69; Emily Writing
   Love 75; Emily's Poems: Charlotte's Editorial 82;
   Wuthering Heights 84

FOUR: EMILY IN NATURE   89
   At Home on the Moors 93; Seasons and Stars 96;
   Animal Bonds 106

FIVE: EMILY AND FEMINISM   117
   Emily's Masculinity 120; Feminist Heights 127

SIX: EMILY'S AFTERLIVES   133
   Beyond the Heights 134; Emily Reimagined 140;
   No Longer Invisible 145

SEVEN: EMILY – REAL AND FAKE NEWS   151

NOTES & REFERENCES   169

SELECTED BIBLIOGRAPHY   179

INDEX   180

ACKNOWLEDGEMENTS   183

This book is dedicated to
the memory of my mum, Margaret,
and to Ted.

INTRODUCTION

The church and parsonage at Haworth, 1857.

What is it about Emily Brontë that continues to fascinate us in the 21st century? For a woman who lived such a short life (she died aged just thirty years old), wrote only one novel, and published a small fraction of poetry in her lifetime (twenty-one poems, to be exact), she holds a remarkably durable place in modern culture. And Emily's legacy can be found everywhere. A quick Google search identifies 'about 4,320,000' results associated with her, returning everything from educational resources, blogs by fans and enthusiasts, social media (yes, of course Emily has her own Twitter account!), official heritage merchandise (sold by the Brontë Parsonage Museum) and quirky home décor for sale, including a knitted 'Emily' doll.

A more visceral modern experience, meanwhile, can be found in 'The Most Wuthering Heights Day Ever', an occasion that's held annually at locations across the globe. It celebrates Emily's novel, *Wuthering Heights* (1847), alongside Kate Bush's 1978 ethereal pop song, which was inspired by the book, and was number one in the UK chart for four weeks. The event climax is a synchronised sing-along and dance to Bush's track. To maximise one's 'wuthering', attendees must learn the choreography from Kate's video, arriving with a red, billowy Cathy dress (that can be homemade or purchased by an authorised 'Cathy' vendor) and be ready to dance. How wonderful!

Thanks to Emily, even my dog can find spiritual serenity through a canine rendition of Emily's famous novel. *Woofering Heights*, a literary-inspired hallucinogenic film produced by More Than Insurance and accessible on YouTube, attempts to soothe upset canines (from fireworks and the like) into a state of meditative contemplation by way of relaxing visuals and a pooch-friendly interpretation of the text narrated by former Doctor Who, David Tenant.

Could Emily's legacy be any more surreal? These objects and events are markers of Emily's place in the 21st century, especially through popular culture. But with such an eclectic and wide-ranging form, it's no wonder that the literary critic Terry Eagleton remarked that 'The Brontës, like Shakespeare, are a literary industry as well as a collection of literary texts'.[1] I wonder what Emily, the so-called reclusive Brontë, might make of her legacy?

Charlotte, Emily's older sister and the pioneering author of *Jane Eyre* (1847), would, I think, be delighted to be a household name and modern cultural phenomenon, for as she confided in a letter to the Poet Laureate Robert Southey in March 1837, she wanted 'to be forever known'.[2] Today not only does a painting of Charlotte (by George Richmond, c. 1850) hang in the National Portrait Gallery in London, but the family's Yorkshire home, Haworth Parsonage, is a pilgrimage destination for thousands of people who travel from all over the globe each year to peek inside the house where the siblings lived and wrote their classic novels.

However, I suspect Emily would be horrified by all things Brontëana. The idea of fans visiting her home and the moors that inspired her work would probably shock her. That tourists now gaze on her image, visible in her brother Branwell's 'Pillar' portrait (c. 1834, also in the National Portrait Gallery), or purchase objects bearing her likeness, would leave her aghast; for Emily, unlike Charlotte, valued her privacy highly and took it rather seriously. As Charlotte indicates in her (in)famous introductory remarks to the 1850 edition of *Wuthering Heights*, her younger sibling 'shunned fame', and desperately wished to remain behind her literary pseudonym of 'Ellis Bell', which was the pen name she wrote under when *Wuthering Heights* was first published (see Chapter Two).

In many ways, Emily's fiercely guarded privacy means that she repels 'investigation as fiercely as Heathcliff rebuffs those to dare to intrude upon his solitude at *Wuthering Heights*'.[3] With this in mind, I guess this makes fans, scholars and enthusiasts a bit like Mr Lockwood in the opening of Emily's novel, who, despite his politeness to Heathcliff – 'I hope I have not inconvenienced you by my perseverance in soliciting the occupation of Thrushcross Grange' – clearly *has* intruded on his landlord's privacy.[4] That said, if Emily would be horrified by her cultural afterlife, I imagine that Keeper, her beloved bullmastiff dog, would approve of the canine reworking of his mistress's canonical text. No doubt the soothing sounds would aid his infamous slumbers on the newly made beds upstairs in Haworth Parsonage (something he did repeatedly, much to the consternation of the Brontës' cook and housekeeper, Tabitha 'Tabby' Aykroyd).

Yet despite Emily's attempt to resist public attention, 200 years after her birth she *still* captivates us. Why? One reason is that Emily's often seen as elusive, and that very inability to pin her down means she is continually sought out. Far less is known about Emily than Charlotte because many of her early and private writings have been mislaid or destroyed (burned, as many have speculated, by Charlotte). Alongside her only novel and surviving poetry, there's literally a handful of perfunctory notes, some sketches, four 'Diary Papers' that she wrote with Anne, a handful of essays written during her time in Belgium (known as the *devoirs*) and the objects of her writing desk to muse over. These precious items form the entirety of primary material that any Emily biographer has to go on, and they are the basis on which her literary legacy rests. We're not even sure what she looked like, and there's debate about some of the details of her likeness. Branwell's 'Pillar' portrait is the only accepted image of her and while it has its merits, it's not entirely realist. Even the portrait used on the cover of this book, which is captioned 'Emily Jane Brontë', is disputed as an authentic portrait (see Chapter Seven).[5]

With so little bequeathed to us directly from Emily, we've naturally come to rely on alternatives to inform us about her, mostly Charlotte's reminiscences of her sister as expressed in her letters and in the opening pages of the 1850 edition of *Wuthering Heights*, but also the anecdotes of family, servants and acquaintances. Elizabeth Gaskell's early account of Emily in *The Life of Charlotte Brontë* (1857) is of significance, too, and I'll discuss this in Chapter Two. But it's worth noting that she never met Emily in person, so her view was also mediated by Charlotte. Such a small body of material makes Emily far less accessible than Charlotte, who, by contrast, left hundreds of letters in addition to several classic novels and a body of poetry behind her.

Emily also continues to captivate the modern imagination because the void in detail about Emily *from* Emily makes her riper for myth-making that any other Brontë. In Emily's case, modern-day medicine and science has been used virulently to portray her as psychologically abnormal: posthumously offering multiple diagnoses of personality disorders and disabilities in order to offer a 'better' understanding of what Charlotte described as her sister's 'unbending' spirit.[6] These reports often interpret Emily on scant details that scramble fact with speculation. Yet each new interpretation promises to deliver a new understanding or truth about Emily. This book will look at some of these allegations, but suffice to note here that whether these ideas are true or untrue (we'll never know) they add to an already tangled web of conjecture about this seemingly 'unknowable' Brontë.

A final reason why Emily continues to enchant audiences lies in the powerful yet enigmatic obscurity of her literary imagination, captured most fully in *Wuthering Heights*. The literary critic F.R. Leavis summarised the power of Emily's novel in his book *The Great Tradition* in 1948, where he heralded Emily as a 'genius' and celebrated the text as an 'astonishing work'.[7] This response is echoed again and again by those who admire Emily's only novel and who find commonality in sharing with others their own experience of reading the text for the first time.[8] I'm no exception to this, so humour me.

My first reading of *Wuthering Heights* left me fascinated by Emily, but with many questions about the nature of the author. I had gobbled up all things Brontë as a teenager after reading Charlotte's *Jane Eyre*; I fell in love with Jane's ardent feminism and delighted in the novel's Gothic sensationalism. But when it came to *Wuthering Heights*, I was perplexed by the depiction of an isolated and violent world. I loved the imagery of the story, especially the wild moorland location over which the tale of class-crossed love unfolds, but I didn't really like many of the characters and found contradictions among them. I'm still not that fond of most of them. And I definitely didn't experience 'Heathcliff mania' as so many other readers do. I felt that the level of violence Heathcliff perpetrates was hugely troubling, and I couldn't understand why this rather demonic male lead (sorry, Heathcliff-ites) was celebrated as a romantic figure.

But irrespective of my trouble with Heathcliff, what struck me the most about the novel was the insistence of Emily's narrative. *Wuthering Heights* wasn't the sort of book you could romp through in one sitting; this powerful drama *commanded* my attention. I still have the same intense reading experience every time I return to it, but it is the novel's imaginative power

– and the fact that each reading reveals something new – that
has made me revisit it repeatedly over the years.

Such literary intensity I later found in Emily's poetry, too.
Like Charlotte, when she first discovered her sister's poems, I
am often blown away by the quality of Emily's writing. Of all of
Emily's poems, I remain mesmerised by one piece in particular:
'No coward soul is mine' (1846):

> *No coward soul is mine*
> *No trembler in the world's storm-troubled sphere*
> *I see Heaven's glories shine*
> *And Faith shines equal arming me from Fear*
>
> *O God within my breast*
> *Almighty ever-present Deity*
> *Life, that in me hast rest,*
> *As I Undying Life, have power in Thee*
>
> *Vain are the thousand creeds*
> *That move men's hearts, unutterably vain,*
> *Worthless as withered weeds*
> *Or idlest froth amid the boundless main*
>
> *To waken doubt in one*
> *Holding so fast by thy infinity,*
> *So surely anchored on*
> *The steadfast rock of Immortality.*
>
> *With wide-embracing love*
> *Thy spirit animates eternal years*
> *Pervades and broods above,*
> *Changes, sustains, dissolves, creates and rears*

> *Though earth and moon were gone*
> *And suns and universes ceased to be*
> *And thou wert left alone*
> *Every Existence would exist in thee*
>
> *There is not room for Death*
> *Nor atom that his might could render void*
> *Since thou art Being and Breath*
> *And what thou art may never be destroyed.*

Essentially, this is a poem about the perseverance of faith. The speaker articulates her relationship with God and describes a view of her soul, telling us that she's unafraid of anything because her faith in Heaven prevents any fear. What courage! Yet what strikes me most about the poem is the speaker's tone of voice, and I imagine it to be Emily. The opening line always raises goosebumps on my arm because it's energetic, authoritative and tremendously brave. As a young feminist, the powerful expression of equality in this piece made a huge impression on me and I wondered: if, potentially, this is how Emily Brontë thought of herself (if indeed it is her speaking), what other powerful feminist comments did she make?

Off I went to the library. But when I read various biographies, what greeted me was not *my* Emily, a defiant woman with confidence in her own sense of self; instead, I found an Emily who was perceived as a mystery, an 'isolated [,] brooding precocious genius' and a repressed 'unfeminine' spinster.[9] In reading about why she was said to be all of these derogatory things, I became frustrated. This was only part of the picture, surely? And Emily's personality and character didn't seem so deviant to me. So what, I thought, if she was unconventional

8

and didn't much like to socialise? So what if she didn't conform to a prescribed notion of what's 'ladylike'? And why do people get so upset that she found vast value in animals and wildlife but didn't care much for Victorian society?

Thankfully, I wasn't alone in questioning why Emily's resistance to convention was continually perceived as wild. But it's only recently that I found a brief echo of my own defensive thoughts about her written by Anne Brontë's latest biographer, Samantha Ellis, who expressed a similar cynicism towards these judgmental views. 'Under pressure to stop whistling, dress fashionably and walk small, no wonder she tried to ignore reality,' said Ellis.[10] Exactly, I thought.

Emily Brontë Reappraised, then, is a biography of sorts with a twist. It revisits some of the dominant ideas that have formed about Emily and reads her afresh from the vantage point of the new millennium. If Emily Brontë was a mystery in her own time, or indeed was a woman ahead of her time, this book considers whether contemporary culture can help us to understand her better and see her anew. In rethinking all that's been written about this shy Brontë sibling, I make no promise of new dramatic revelations about the facts of Emily's life. In fact, I'm going to look at what we *do* know about Emily to conjure a new image based on biography, her writings and her afterlives. Throughout the book, excerpts from the surviving materials left by Emily are included and it is my hope that these sources situate what we do have of Emily's voice at the centre of the book. So, 200 years on, then, amidst all the hustle and bustle of the 21st century, let's see if the 'real' Emily Brontë can now stand up.

This book begins with a capsule history of Emily's life, establishing the facts about this apparently 'unknowable' Brontë. Chapter One isn't meant to be an exhaustive account; rather, it's an overview of the important moments and relationships that came to shape her as an adult. I hope to show here that we do know quite a lot more about Emily than we often think. As a helpful addition to this summary, the chapter includes a chronological overview of the main events of Emily's life in the context of her immediate family.

Chapter Two explores what others have said about Emily and takes a closer look at how she's been portrayed in biography. As well as summarising the differing viewpoints, this chapter focuses primarily on points of tension and disagreement between sources in order to show just how many different Emilys exist. How truthful are these accounts and do they matter? And, most importantly, how relevant are they in revisiting Emily today?

Chapter Three looks with fresh eyes at the trajectory of Emily's writing career and thinks about how her writings inform our understanding of her. The discussion presents edited snapshots of Emily's imagination, teasing out some of the ways in which her writings reveal important insights into her priorities, concerns, politics and creativity and how these connect to the modern world.

Chapter Four turns to the subject of nature, a topic that's witnessed a resurgence in recent years, thanks to the likes of David Attenborough, Chris Packham and the scores of passionate and highly talented nature writers from the UK alone. Although associated with the entire Brontë family, the moors have a special place in writings about Emily because they signify so much about her and her relationship with the natural world, including animals and wildlife. Drawing primarily on Emily's poetry – her authorised poetic collection from 1846 and the remnants of her fantasy 'Gondal' writings – as well her Belgian *devoirs*, this chapter asks how relevant is Emily's passion for the natural world in a time of heightened environmental awareness?

The next chapter examines Emily's view(s) towards gender, making the case that she was indeed a staunch feminist (which will be contentious for some). It's interesting that Emily has often been criticised as being 'unwomanly' and was described on more than one occasion as 'masculine'. In her own time, such charges would have horrified many and been equated with deviance. Today, modern readers are more likely to wonder what the big deal is. Accordingly, this chapter revisits some of what has been said about Emily's feminism (or proto-feminism, to be precise, since the term didn't come into usage until much later in the century) and reshapes the material in light of contemporary feminism. It also offers some new thoughts on *Wuthering Heights* informed by recent feminist concerns, making the case for Emily as a feminist ahead of her time.

Chapter Six explores Emily's 'literary afterlives', including biofiction and adaptations. It begins with a focus on 21st-century remakes of *Wuthering Heights* and considers how Emily's novel has been made amenable to modern audiences. It examines numerous 'rewrites' of the text with a focus on modern-day issues, ranging from questions of race and multiculturalism, through to sex and S&M (because yes, of course her work has been eroticised). In the latter part of the chapter, I move onto representations of the author herself in biofiction and biodrama. Beginning with Charlotte's portrayal of Emily in *Shirley* (1849), where Emily is the titular Shirley, I begin to flesh out how she's been reimagined in creative fiction since the 19th century.

As a final means of placing Emily in the new millennium, the last chapter maps some of the real and 'fake news' stories that are associated with her, considering both the sane and silly to try to reclaim Emily (so to speak) amidst masses of disputatious writings that surround the Brontës. 'Fake news' is a decidedly 21st-century term, but Brontë myth-making, as the scholar Lucasta Miller has persuasively shown, can be traced back to the Brontës' own time.

ONE

THE LIFE AND WORKS OF EMILY

Another portrait widely claimed to be of Emily that is of uncertain origin and dubious likeness (known as the Getty Portrait).

THE EARLY YEARS

Emily Jane Brontë was born on 30 July 1818 at her father's parsonage at Thornton in Bradford. She was the fifth child of Patrick and Maria Brontë, being four years younger than the eldest child, Maria, three years younger than the second child, Elizabeth, two years younger than Charlotte, a year younger than her only brother Branwell, and one year older than the baby of the family, Anne.

Shortly before Emily's second birthday, the family relocated to the parsonage in Haworth that still stands at the top of the cobbled main street. At this time, Haworth was a busy industrial town with approximately 4,700 inhabitants, many of whom worked at the local textile and woollen mills. But then it was also a tough place to live. Ill health there was aggravated by the poor quality of the water, which was so bad even the cattle are said to have refused it. Residents, crammed into small living quarters, threw all waste (everything from offal and ashes to the refuse of privies) into small enclosures in their backyards, and many households – the parsonage excluded – had to share privies.[1] With ill health dominating the lives of so many in the community, it is no wonder that Patrick Brontë was a terribly busy man.

To some extent, the Brontës were largely isolated from the village, for apart from 'dealings with Patrick's curates', they 'did not mix on equal terms with the textile workers, shopkeepers, and tradesman of their households'.[2] But health issues don't discriminate by class, and the Brontë family was affected too to devastating effect. Within a year of the family's arrival in Haworth, Maria, Emily's mother, became ill with uterine cancer. She died in 1821 when Emily was just three years old, a terribly young age to suffer such a shattering life event. Undoubtedly it would have been a traumatic experience. Certainly, in one of her later poems, an untitled one written in 1840, the adult speaker reflects on the recognition that in their earlier years they were fortunate to have a loved one (now departed) for the period that they did:

> *It is too late to call thee now –*
> *I will not nurse that dream again*
> *For every joy that lit my brow*
> *Would bring its after-storm of pain*
>
> *Besides the mist is half withdrawn,*
> *The barren mountain-side lies bare*
> *And sunshine and awaking morn*
> *Paint no more golden visions there –*
>
> *Yet ever in my grateful breast*
> *Thy darling shade shall cherished be*
> *For God alone doth know how blest*
> *My early years have been in thee!*[3]

After her mother's passing, Maria, the eldest daughter, then aged seven, assumed responsibility for her younger siblings, acting in her mother's place, while two local girls, Nancy and Sarah Garrs, were employed as housekeeper and nursemaid for them. The children's aunt, Elizabeth Branwell – better known colloquially as 'Aunt Branwell' – who had cared for her sister during her illness, also decided to remain at the parsonage. In the wake of her sister's death, she took on a pseudo-parental role alongside Patrick.

A few years later, aged just six, Emily left home for the first time, following her elder sisters to the Clergy Daughters' School

at Cowan Bridge, the institution Charlotte famously reconstructed as the miserable Lowood School in *Jane Eyre*. Emily's
school record isn't remarkable and doesn't capture any of the
genius that F.R. Leavis later attributed to her, but it's fascinating
due to this very point, for it grossly underestimates the ability of
this would-be prodigy. It reads: 'Emily Brontë. Entered Nov. 25,
1824. Aged 5¾. Reads very prettily and Works a little. Left School
June 1, 1825. Subsequent career, governess.'[4] Clearly she didn't
impress whoever compiled the register. In *Jane Eyre*, Charlotte is
explicit about the miserly conditions at Lowood:

> *Our clothing was insufficient to protect us from the severe
> cold; we had no boots, the snow got into our shoes, and
> melted there; our ungloved hands became numbed and
> covered with chilblains, as were our feet [...] Then the
> scanty supply of food was distressing: with the keen appe-
> tites of growing children, we had scarcely sufficient to keep
> alive a delicate invalid.*[5]

Despite these rather abject circumstances, we do know that
Emily was at least looked on favourably at Cowan Bridge. The
school's superintendent, Miss Anne Evans, fondly recalled 'little
petted Em', the 'darling child' and 'pet nursling' of the school.[6]
But Emily was only there five months. Her departure came about
as a result of a typhoid epidemic that ravaged the school, leading to the decline of her sisters, who were caught up in it and
soon sent home suffering from tuberculosis. Maria returned to
Haworth in February 1825 and spent three months convalesc-
ing, but the disease proved too much. She died on 6 May. Three
weeks later, on 31 May, Elizabeth returned home too, but her
demise was even faster than Maria's; she died on 15 June.

What might surprise a modern-day reader about the three

successive familial losses is that the Brontë's situation was not unusual: it was in keeping with the high mortality rates in Haworth. Death rates in the village 'rivalled those in London', with more than forty-one per cent of children dying before their sixth birthday and the average age of death being just twenty-five.[7] So, that the remaining children survived into adulthood, and Patrick Brontë lived well into his elder years, is really quite remarkable.

We don't know if Emily had specific recollections of her sibling's deaths, although Denise Giardina's recent novel based on Emily's life, *Emily's Ghost: A Novel of the Brontë Sisters* (2009) reimagines her closeness with her sisters and constructs her in a *Sixth Sense*-y manner, seeing and speaking with Elizabeth when she passed (see also Chapter Seven). Nonetheless, it's more than reasonable to assume that following so soon after the loss of their mother, Maria and Elizabeth's passing 'broke another link in the family'.[8] Numerous Brontë scholars have described how the rapid loss of the sisters collectively impacted on the remaining children.

It was not simply that they had lost two of their sisters, but that they lost their two eldest sisters. The younger children had naturally looked to them for the leadership and support that elder children provide. In their case this role had taken on even greater importance because Maria, and to a lesser extent Elizabeth, had taken on maternal roles in their lives after the death of their mother.

In this context, it seems perfectly understandable that Patrick Brontë didn't want to send his remaining daughters back to the school where his eldest children had become fatally ill. So, for the next four years, Charlotte and Emily stayed at home in Haworth with Branwell and Anne. Contrary to reports by Elizabeth Gaskell in *The Life of Charlotte Brontë*, the family environment at the parsonage was a happy one, as this account of a typical day for the children from Juliet Barker's authoritative biography, *The Brontës* (1994), describes. Their days began with the whole family, including the servant staff,

> assembling in Patrick's study for prayers. The children then accompanied him [...] for a 'plain but abundant' breakfast [and] were then committed to Sarah's care till dinner-time [.] While Patrick went out to do his parish visiting in the afternoon, the children walked out on the moors everyday unless the weather was too bad. These walks were the highlight of their day [...] On their return home they found tea waiting for them [.] Patrick came in later and [...] gathered the children about him 'for recitation and talk, giving them oral lessons in history, biography or travel'.[9]

The image Barker describes is warm, comforting and pleasant. It also elucidates the kind of parent Patrick was, far removed from the violent and dismissive figure Elizabeth Gaskell portrayed him as. Here we see Patrick's close involvement with his children's daily routine, meeting them for prayers in the morning and spending quality time together in the evening. Biblical reading and study was also an important part of the day, and Patrick used religious teaching to strengthen parent–child bonds, something apparent in his gift of an Oxford Bible to Emily in 1827. His inscription inside one of the family Bibles lovingly reads: 'To Emily Jane Brontë, by her affectionate Father, February 13, 1827'. Furthermore, while it's not mentioned in this particular extract, we know that Emily also learned music (she played the piano) and she enjoyed drawing.

The children's days may have been structured, but as Barker shows, it was their leisure time that they loved the most. Emily's love of nature, expressed in so much of her writing, can be traced back to her childhood days wildly romping about on the moors. One occasion clearly left an impression on her. In September 1824, when she was just six, Emily was with Branwell and Anne under the watchful eye of teenage servants, Nancy and Sarah Garrs, when a bog erupted behind the parsonage at Crow Hill during a sensational storm. Patrick was frantic about his children's welfare, not realising that they had all reached safety in a porch of nearby Ponden Hall in time to watch the spectacular natural event. The sight of boulders being thrown up into the air and a seven-foot high wave of mud, peat and water exploding and sweeping all the way down the hillside amazed the young Emily. But this was also a very serious natural disaster caused, as was later discovered, by an earthquake that created a landslip and flooding. Patrick bravely ran out to rescue his children, risking his own life, and he eventually found them quivering and hiding under Sarah's cloak. Twelve years later, in December 1836, Emily, aged eighteen, wrote of the bog-burst in a poem:

> *High waving heather 'neath stormy blasts bending*
> *Midnight and moonlight and bright shining stars*
> *Darkness and glory rejoicingly blending*
> *Earth rising to heaven and heaven descending*
> *Man's spirit away from its drear dungeon sending,*
> *Bursting the fetters and breaking the bars.*
>
> *All down the mountain sides wild forests lending*
> *One mighty voice to the life-giving wind*
> *Rivers their banks in their jubilee rending*
> *Fast through the valleys a reckless course wending*
> *Wider and deeper their waters extending*
> *Leaving a desolate desert behind*

Shining and lowering and swelling and dying
Changing forever from midnight to noon
Roaring like thunder, like soft music sighing
Shadows on shadows advancing and flying
Lightning bright flashes the deep gloom defying
Coming as swiftly and fading as soon.[10]

The poem was never titled, but it's clear that the breathtaking sight left its mark on the impressionable young Brontë. The power of the natural world is something Emily repeatedly describes in her creative writings and very often, as in this poem, man is no match for its grandeur.

Emily never went back to school as a young child and so, apart from the brief period she spent at Cowan Bridge, her formal education was minimal. Instead, throughout the years, she was guided on general matters and domestic rudiments by Aunt Branwell, and on religious matters by her father. She gained self-instruction from 'personal observation' and the resources at her disposal at the parsonage, and she gleaned all sorts of other types of 'information from her brothers and sisters'.[11]

Later, aged seventeen, Emily did briefly return to school, joining Charlotte at Miss Wooler's, Roe Head. But whereas Charlotte returned as a teacher, Emily went as a pupil (it was Charlotte's position as a tutor that paid for Emily's education). But the period at Roe Head was not particularly easy for Emily. She disliked the discipline and structure, so she returned home after three months and was replaced by Anne.

The other important thing to note about Emily as a child is how she thrived in the home environment. With free access to her father's bookshelves, she rapidly devoured all the materials that he brought home. And, like her siblings, she showed the same interest in history, politics, literature and current news events reported in local newspapers and sources like *Blackwood's Magazine*. From this reading, Emily's early childhood heroes emerged. Sir Walter Scott, a favourite of all the Brontës, was particularly beloved by Emily, and she received her own copy of one of the books in his *Tales of a Grandfather* series (1827–1829) from Aunt Branwell in 1828.

Byron was also among her favourites, and many scholars have usefully traced the echoes of Byron's poems in Emily's own work, suggesting that she was very familiar with a whole range of his poetry. Staying with the Romantics, poems by Shelley and Wordsworth were also avidly devoured in the parsonage.

Such eclectic reading fuelled Emily's imagination, and its impact was soon to become significant, for it was about to find expression in the fantasy stories that she began to co-create with her brother and sisters.

During the 1820s and '30s, artists were increasingly depicting nature's moods and power, as in this 1836 JMW Turner painting of the River Tees, Yorkshire.

TOY SOLDIERS

It's often said that the Brontë children's isolation made them dependent on each other and certainly this is true, but this dependence also opened up wildly creative literary talents. In 1826, Patrick Brontë returned home from a clergy conference in Leeds with a box of toy soldiers for Branwell. The children were hugely excited by the colourful box of twelve wooden figures and Charlotte captured their youthful exhilaration in a diary paper from 1829:

> Papa brought Branwell some soldiers in Leeds. When Papa came home it was night we were in bed so next morning Branwell came to our door with a box of soldiers. Emily and I jumped out of bed and I snatched up one and exclaimed this is the Duke of Wellington it shall be mine!! When I said this Emily likewise took one and said it should be hers. When Anne came down she took one also. Mine was the prettiest of the whole and perfect in every part. Emily's was a grave looking fellow [and] we called him Gravey. Anne's was a queer little boy thing much like herself. He was called Waiting-Boy. Branwell chose Bonaparte.[12]

Compared to Charlotte and Branwell's figures, Emily's 'grave looking fellow' and Anne's 'queer little boy' sound incredibly dull, but then again, they were only eight and six years old, respectively, *and* they had second pickings. Gravey, however, quickly grew into a more glamorous adventurer, becoming Sir William Edward Parry, so named after the real-life Arctic explorer who commanded five expeditions to the North-West Passage. Accordingly, Parry's real-life companion, John Ross, was assigned as Anne's newly imagined soldier. Emily made Parry the King of 'Parry's Land', a kingdom she modelled on the West Yorkshire countryside. Parry's Land was one of four islands comprising Glass Town, a fictionalised part of West Africa that had the city of Verdopolis as its capital.

Like all children playing with their toys, the Brontës not only gave the toy soldier's names and landscapes; they created huge stories about them as well and acted them out (a bit like Mike and his friends in Netflix's *Stranger Things*, who dramatise their game of *Dungeons and Dragons*). With these particular toys, however, the children decided to imagine their backstories, thus *The History of the Young Men* emerged. Charlotte wrote:

> *Our plays were established; Young Men, June, 1826; Our Fellows, July, 1827; Islanders, December, 1827. These are our three great plays, that are not kept secret. ...The Young Men's play took its rise from some wooden soldiers Branwell had; Our Fellows from Æsop's Fables; and the Islanders from several events which happened. I will sketch out the origin of our plays more explicitly if I can.*[13]

These dramas were so important that the children made efforts to preserve them, writing them down in tiny handmade books (measuring less than thirteen centimetres square) formed from scraps of paper sewn into covers made from various household items, such as sugar bags, parcel wrapping and wallpaper, amongst other things.

As the stories began to consume the children's everyday lives, the fantasy landscapes grew. Charlotte later spoke of how she and Emily would continue to write in secret at night, creating dramas from the historical and political events that absorbed them; their 'bed plays', she called them.[14]

From these 'humble' beginnings, then, the world of Angria was born. From 1829, Charlotte and Branwell became the leaders in the games the children played about Glass Town and Angria, and Emily and Anne were Chief Genii (as their roles were termed), directing the actions of Parry and Ross. The stories they all created described the many feuds, loves, politics, imprisonments and domestic sagas of their imaginary worlds. Gradually, however, the youngest children's interests changed from those that excited Charlotte and Branwell, so when Charlotte initially left home to attend Roe Head school in January 1831, the younger Brontës seized the opportunity to break from the collective Glass Town and Angrian sagas to form their own kingdom a rebel spin-off called Gondal.

Located in the Pacific, Gondal was an all-female kingdom (see Chapter Five). Not much of the material about it survives, but Emily's published poems from 1846 were largely derived from the saga; she merely edited out reference to it. What's particularly important about Gondal is that even after her literary career was formed, Emily never stopped writing about this world. She returned to it repeatedly over the years right up until her death in 1848.

DIARY PAPERS

Emily and Anne's newly created adjunct world brought them closer together than they had ever been. Ellen Nussey, Charlotte's life-long friend, later described the pair as 'like twins, inseparable companions, and in the very closet sympathy which never had any interruption'.[15] Importantly, from November 1834, the sisters began collaborating on their Diary Papers, brief yearly records of domestic life and family affairs that they wrote (mainly) on their birthdays until 1845. The first paper was written by Emily on 24 November 1834. It's fairly lengthy, but its delightful mundanity reveals much about the pair. It reads:

I fed Rainbow, Diamond Snowflake Jasper pheasant (alias) this morning Branwell went down to Mr. Driver's and brought news that Sir Robert Peel was going to be invited to stand for Leeds Anne and I have been peeling apples for Charlotte to make us an apple pudding and for Aunt nuts and apples Charlotte said she made puddings perfectly and she was of a quick but limited intellect. Taby said just now Come Anne pilloputate (i.e. pill a potato) Aunt has come into the kitchen just now and said where are your feet Anne Anne answered On the floor Aunt papa opened the parlour door and gave Branwell a letter saying here Branwell read this and show it to your Aunt and Charlotte–The Gondals are discovering the interior of Gaaldine Sally Mosley is washing in the back kitchen

It is past Twelve o'clock Anne and I have not tidied ourselves, done our bedwork or done our lessons and we want to go out to play we are going to have for Dinner Boiled Beef, Turnips, potatoes and applepudding. The Kitchin is in a very untidy state Anne and I have not done our music exercise which consists of b major Taby said on my putting a pen in her face Ya pitter pottering there instead of pilling a potate I answered O Dear, O Dear, O dear I will directly with that I get up, take a knife and begin pilling (finished) pilling the potatoes papa going to walk Mr. Sunderland expected.

Anne and I say I wonder what we shall be like and what we shall be and where we shall be if all goes on well in the year 1874–in which year I shall be in my 54th year Anne will be going in her 55th year Branwell will be going in his 58th year And Charlotte in her 59th year hoping we shall all be well at that time we close our paper.

The terrible spelling and tenuous grasp of punctuation here are all Emily's, but the textual chaos adds to an otherwise happy domestic scene. Emily, we see, is peeling potatoes and apples with Anne, but with Charlotte's arrival a competitive edge emerges thanks to the latter's comment on the perfected nature of her own apple pudding. Notably, the siblings are honest about how they slack in other domestic responsibilities: 'bedwork', lessons and music practice and the carelessness is affirmed by the sketches and scribbles that frame the page, showing how relaxed the sisters are in the kitchen.

Importantly, this first paper also provides us with a glimpse into Emily's (and Anne's) creative mind, for amidst all the business of the domestic she references Gondal, describing what aspect of the saga she was working on at that time: the interior of Gaaldine. The spilling over of fantasy into the real world gave Emily huge pleasure and it's something she would continue to do all her life. In the Diary Paper entry from 1845, for example, Emily describes the recent trip she made with Anne to York, during which the sisters 'enjoyed' pretending to be prisoners 'escaping from the Palaces of Instruction to join the Royalists who are hard driven at present by the victorious Republicans' for the duration of the journey.[16]

Returning to their first Diary Paper, however, the other important thing to note is how it captures something of Emily's sense of humour (a trait she's definitely *not* usually associated with). Emily teases Tabby by constructing her Yorkshire dialect in prose, something she would go on to do later in *Wuthering Heights* in her portrayal of Joseph. Indeed, her humour is something I'm fascinated by and I'll return to it at points in the book.

GROWING PAINS

Despite her lack of formal education, Emily was determined to earn a living on her own terms. In September 1838, aged twenty, she accepted a post as teacher at Law Hill school in Halifax, much to Charlotte's consternation: 'Hard labour from six in the morning until near eleven at night with only one hour of exercise between – this is slavery I fear she will never stand it.'[17] Emily had forty pupils at Law Hill and while she was not unpopular with them, the feeling was not reciprocated. One of her pupils recalled that she informed them that the house-dog was 'dearer to her than they were', but then this is unsurprising given her fondness for animals (see also Chapter Five).[18] Indeed, Emily found little pleasure in the formality of learning and education at Law Hill, and by her second term, her happiness and health had deteriorated. Charlotte reported that this was because Emily became homesick: 'The change from her own home to a school, and from her own very noiseless, very secluded, but unrestricted and unartificial mode of life, to one of disciplined routine (though under the kindest auspices), was what she failed in enduring.'[19] This extract (the first five stanzas) from a poem she wrote on 4 December 1838 idealise her love for home. It's known as 'A little while, a little while':

> *A little while, a little while*
> *The noisy crowd are barred away;*
> *And I can sing and I can smile*
> *A little while I've holiday!*
>
> *Where wilt thou go my harassed heart?*
> *Full many a land invites thee now;*

And places near, and far apart
Have rest for thee, my weary brow –

There is a spot 'mid barren hills
Where winter howls and driving rain
But if the dreary tempest chills
There is a light that warms again

The house is old, the trees are bare
And moonless bends the misty dome
But what on earth is half so dear –
So longed for the hearth of home?

The mute bird singing on the stone
The dank-moss dripping from the wall,
The garden-walk with weeds o'ergrown
I love them – how I love them all![20]

In such an unhappy state of mind, Emily made the decision to return home. There she resumed her education, learning Latin with her father and translating Virgil's *Aeneid* and Horace's *Ars Poetica*, and reading the Four Gospels. She also renewed her passion for drawing, sketching vigorously from images in magazines and manuals, including Thomas Bewick's *A History of British Birds* (1797), the book that Jane Eyre reads secretly when curled up in the window seat in the library in chapter one of Charlotte's novel.

It's during this period that Charlotte concocted a plan that would enable the sisters to remain socially and financially independent; she suggested that they set up a school of their own, the 'Miss Brontës Establishment for the Board and Education of a limited number of Young Ladies'. Charlotte even had some publicity cards drawn up for it. But to realise this idea, the sisters would have to polish particular aspects of their own education. Emily was keen to improve her language skills and thus agreed to accompany Charlotte to Brussels, where they enrolled at the Pensionnat Héger, an 'Educational Establishment for Young Ladies'.

Gaskell famously wrote of this experience that the sisters 'wanted learning. They came for learning. They would learn', and so they did.[21] In a letter to her friend Ellen Nussey, Charlotte described how Emily worked 'like a horse' to improve her French, but unfortunately, she and the school's master, M. Constantin Héger, did not get on well.[22] Emily disliked Héger's teaching methods, fearing that her originality might be lost from being forced to compose in various models requested by her tutor. For his part, Héger later recalled how Emily objected 'strongly – and vocally' to his teaching methods, but his approach paid off. Later, he claimed that he 'saw the genius' in Emily's writing, and he chose to preserve some of her *devoirs*.[23] But Emily's 'head for logic' and a strong ability to argue in prose form was, Héger believed, undermined by her 'stubborn tenacity of will, which rendered her obtuse to all reasoning where own wishes, or her own sense of right, was concerned'.[24] In other words, Emily was independent.

Aside from her educational development, Emily's time in Brussels was not a very happy one. She spent time with Joseph and Mary Taylor, two of Charlotte's close friends, but she was generally disinterested in the small English community there. Several sources reported that she rarely spoke in public, which may well be true given that in '*Le Chat*' (The Cat), one of her *devoirs*, Emily suggests that politeness in humans is little more than hypocrisy. Small talk clearly wasn't for her.

The sisters' time in Brussels came to a sudden end with news of the death of Aunt Branwell. When they returned from the Continent, Emily discovered she had been bequeathed £300 from her aunt. Such a sum of money relieved her of any immediate pressure to develop a teaching career, and so Emily decided not to return to Europe with her sister. Instead, she opted to assume responsibility for the housekeeping in the parsonage.

Emily's place may have been firmly located in the domestic sphere, but her decision afforded her control over her own time. She could continue to widen her knowledge of various subjects and write until her heart was content, as long as she fulfilled her duties, of course. In later years, servants would report to biographers their memories of Emily working in the kitchen, recalling how she always had a book in hand as she worked, both to read (we know she was learning German) and to make notes.

Being at home clearly opened up Emily's creative drive, and in 1844 she began to separate her poems into two different notebooks: a Gondal one and a non-Gondal one. It was in 1845 that Charlotte discovered Emily's poems and persuaded her sister, eventually, to publish them in a joint volume with material by Charlotte and Anne. The sisters assumed pseudonyms – Currer, Ellis and Acton Bell – for the publication of the anthology, and although it only sold two copies, there was much critical praise for Emily's writings.

Hot off the heels of her first publication, Emily set to work in earnest on her novel, *Wuthering Heights*, and following nightly writing sessions in the dining room of the parsonage, the text was published jointly with Anne's *Agnes Grey* in 1847. Based on comments in a letter from her publisher, in which he tells her not to hurry too fast with 'your next novel' there are suggestions that Emily had begun writing a second novel at this time, but sadly, if she did, no manuscript has ever been found.[25]

FINAL DAYS

Concurrently, during this period of domesticity and creativity for Emily, Branwell's life began to spiral. By 1845, he had succumbed to alcohol addiction and, it's said, opium. Having failed as a poet, a painter and a tutor, he was also fired from a teaching post at Thorpe Green for allegedly fraternising with the mistress of the house, Lydia Robinson. Their relationship ended rather abruptly after her husband's death. Branwell was not to see Mrs Robinson again; or so the terms of Mr Robinson's will dictated, for if Mrs Robinson entertained him, she would have to forfeit her husband's estate. With his artistic and creative hopes dashed, Branwell turned to substances to numb his pain, working himself into a state of debt (for which collectors regularly visited the parsonage), and soon he became gravely ill.

Branwell died from tuberculosis on 24 September 1848 aged just thirty-one. During the funeral service, Emily displayed the symptoms of a common cold. But this was not a cold; it was the beginnings of tuberculosis. By the end of October 1848, Charlotte confided in Ellen Nussey her fears about Emily's health:

> *Emily's cold and cough are very obstinate. I fear she has pain in the chest – and I sometimes catch a shortness in her breathing when she had moved at all quickly – She looks very, very thin and pale. Her reserved nature occasions one great uneasiness of mind – it is useless to question her – you get no answers – it is still more useless to recommend remedies – they are never adopted.*[26]

A few days later, things had exacerbated. Emily's cough and

cold now appeared 'like a slow inflammation of the lung', but Emily refused help: 'she neither seeks nor will accept sympathy; to put any question, to offer any aid is to annoy … you must look on, and see her do what she is unfit to do, and not dare say a word.'[27] Charlotte tried to persuade her sister to permit some form of therapeutic intervention, pleading with her to try remedies ranging from traditional medicine to homeopathy, which Emily vehemently dismissed as a 'form of Quackery', declaring that 'no poisoning doctor' would come near her.[28] The refusal pained Charlotte deeply. She struggled to watch her sister's health decline and continued to express her anguish to friends.

Tragically, it was on the day of Emily's death that she finally relented to Charlotte's pleas, agreeing for medical aid to attend her. 'If you will send for a Doctor, I will see him now,' she's reported to have whispered to her sisters.[29] Emily Brontë died at home at two o'clock in the afternoon on 19 December 1848 with her dog, Keeper, lying at her side.

A simple burial service took place on 22 December, with a procession led by her father and Keeper, who walked 'first side by side'.[30] The pair led Emily's coffin to her final resting spot, the family vault in St Michael and All Angels' Church in Haworth, where she was 'reunited' with her mother and siblings. Keeper lay 'in the pew couched at our feet while the burial service was being read' and when he returned to the parsonage, he took up post outside Emily's room, 'where he howled pitifully for many days'.[31]

Emily's death was a devastating loss for Charlotte. In a letter to Ellen Nussey on 23 December 1848, in which she informs her friend of her sister's passing, she conveys poignantly her surprise at the speed of Emily's decline:

Emily suffers no more either from pain or weakness now. She never will suffer more in this world. She is gone after a hard, short conflict. She died on Tuesday, the very day I wrote to you. I thought it might be possible then she might be with us still for weeks and a few hours afterwards she was in Eternity.[32]

Two days later, on Christmas Day 1848, she wrote to William Smith Williams, their publisher, conveying the rawness of her grief:

Emily is nowhere here now – her wasted mortal remains are taken out of the house; we have laid her cherished head under the church-aisle beside my mother's my two sisters', dead long ago, and my poor hapless brother's...

Well – the loss is ours – not hers, and some sad comfort I take, as I hear the wind blow and feel the cutting keenness of the frost, in knowing that the elements bring her no more suffering – their severity cannot reach her grave – her fever is quieted, her restless soothed, her deep, hollow cough is hushed for ever; we do not hear it in the night or listen for it in the morning, we have no the conflict of the strangely strong spirit and the fragile frame before us – relentless conflict – once seen, never to be forgotten. A dreary calm reigns around us, in the midst of which we seek resignation...

I will not ask now why Emily was taken from us in the fullness of our attachment, rooted up in the prime of her own days, in the promise of her powers – why her existence now lies like a field of green corn trodden down – like a tree in full bearing – struck at the root. I will only say, sweet is rest after labour and calm after tempest, and repeat again and again that Emily knows that now.[33]

Emily's death was more agonising for Charlotte than Branwell's or Anne's, which came the following May. In a letter to Williams in June 1849, Charlotte described how she 'let Anne go to God and felt He had a right to her', but of Emily she said, 'I could hardly let Emily go – I wanted to hold her back then – and I want her back now.'[34]

In the plethora of commentaries by Charlotte about her sister's passing, it's clear that she never really recovered from Emily's death, and partly this was because she knew that Emily had so much more to give and had died at too young an age. Charlotte was right. But irrespective of the tragedy of Emily's short life, it remains remarkable that by the time she had turned thirty, she had produced a novel that is widely regarded as one of *the* greatest works of English literature. That in itself is a legacy to inspire.

CHRONOLOGY OF EMILY'S LIFE & WORKS

1818   Emily Brontë is born on 30 July. She is the fifth child of the Reverend Patrick Brontë and Maria Branwell, and has four elder siblings; three sisters and one brother.

1820   Anne Brontë is born on 17 January. In April of this year, the family move to the parsonage in Haworth.

1821   Elizabeth Branwell, Emily's aunt, arrives in Haworth to care for her sister. Emily's mother, Maria Brontë, dies aged thirty-eight from cancer on 15 September.

1824   On 25 November, Emily attends the Clergy Daughters' School at Cowan Bridge, following her two eldest sisters, Maria and Elizabeth, who went in July, and Charlotte, who went in August. Tabitha ('Tabby') Aykroyd is engaged as a family servant.

1825   Maria returns home from Cowan Bridge with tuberculosis on 14 February. She dies on 6 May. Elizabeth is sent home in decline on 31 May. Charlotte and Emily return home the next day. Elizabeth dies on 15 June. All the children remain at home until 1830 under the supervision of their aunt, Elizabeth Branwell.

1826   On 5 June, Branwell receives the toy soldiers that lead to the children's creation of the imaginary worlds of Glass Town, Angria and, eventually, Gondal.

1829   The children receive art lessons from John Bradley of Keighley.

1831   Charlotte attends Margaret Wooler's school at Roe Head. There she befriends Ellen Nussey and Mary Taylor, who would become lifelong friends.

1832   Charlotte leaves Roe Head in June.

1833   The Brontës visit Bolton Abbey with the Nusseys.

1834   Emily and Anne write their first Diary Paper, which includes the earliest reference to Gondal.

1835   On 2 July, Charlotte returns to Roe Head as a teacher and Emily joins her as a pupil. In October, Emily returns home from Roe Head and is replaced by Anne.

1836   Emily's first dated poem is written ('Cold clear and blue the morning heaven').

1838   In September, Emily accepts a teaching post at Miss Patchett's school at Law Hill, Halifax.

1839   Emily returns to Haworth from Law Hill in March of this year.

1841   The sisters plan to start a school of their own, possibly at Bridlington. Charlotte asks Aunt Branwell for financial support for her and Emily to perfect their languages in Brussels.

1842   In February, Emily and Charlotte travel to Brussels to enrol at the Pensionnat Héger, school for girls. On 29 October, Aunt Branwell dies suddenly and both sisters return home in early November.

1843   Charlotte returns to Brussels without Emily.

1844   Emily begins transcribing her poems into two notebooks, one entitled *Gondal Poems*, the other untitled.

1845   In June, Anne and Emily travel to York and return in July. In September of that year, Charlotte discovers Emily's poetry and spends two days persuading her sister to seek publication for their poems under pseudonyms.

1846   *Poems by Currer, Ellis and Acton Bell* is published.

1847   In October, Charlotte's *Jane Eyre* is published and widely praised. In December, Emily's only novel, *Wuthering Heights*, is published alongside Anne's *Agnes Grey* as a single edition by Thomas Cautley Newby.

1848   In February, Newby proposes to 'make arrangements' for 'Ellis Bell's next novel', offering advice on the 'new work'. In June, Anne's *The Tenant of Wildfell Hall* is published. Branwell dies on 24 September, aged thirty-one. Emily dies on 19 December, aged thirty.

1849   Anne dies in Scarborough on 28 May, aged twenty-nine. Charlotte's second novel, *Shirley*, is published in October. *Shirley* features an imaginary construction of Emily had she lived.

1850   In August, Charlotte meets Elizabeth Gaskell. In December, Charlotte publishes an edited volume of *Wuthering Heights* and *Agnes Grey* with a 'Biographical Notice' about her sisters.

1852   Arthur Bell Nicholls, her father's curate, asks Charlotte to marry him.

1853   *Villette*, Charlotte's third novel, is published.

1854   Charlotte marries Arthur Bell Nicholls. The couple honeymoon in Ireland.

1855   Charlotte dies on 31 March, aged thirty-eight.

1857   Charlotte's first novel, *The Professor*, is published posthumously. Elizabeth Gaskell's biography, *The Life of Charlotte Brontë*, is published in March.

1861   Patrick dies on 7 June, aged eighty-five.

TWO
EMILY – THE BIOGRAPHERS' TALES

Anne, Emily and Charlotte, as painted by Branwell (who originally appeared as the central, obscured figure), in 1834.

In May 1871, Charlotte's lifelong friend, Ellen Nussey, published her reminiscences of the Brontë family in *Scribner's Monthly*. Recalling the first visit she made to the parsonage in 1833, Ellen conveyed her earliest memory of the then fifteen-year-old Emily:

> *Emily Brontë had by this time acquired a lithesome, grace-ful figure. She was the tallest person in the house, except her father. Her hair, which was naturally as beautiful as Charlotte's, was in the same unbecoming tight curl and frizz, and there was the same want of complexion. She had very beautiful eyes – kind, kindling eyes; but she did not look at you often; she was too reserved. Their colour might be dark grey, at other times dark blue, they varied so. She talked very little.*[1]

Nussey's sketch is, on the whole, rather flattering, but her comment on Emily's eyes is conspicuous for associating Emily's infamous reserve with kindness, a rarity in Brontë biographies. Ellen later elaborated on her comment to Clement King Shorter, one of Charlotte's early biographers, describing how

> *Emily's reserve seemed impenetrable, yet she was intensely loveable; she invited confidence in her moral power. Few people have the gift of looking and smiling as she could look and smile. One of her rare expressive looks was something to remember through life, there was such a depth of soul and feeling, and yet such a shyness of revealing herself.*[2]

This passing remark may seem banal, even trivial, to a modern reader. But for Emily's fans it is significant since she is often remembered rather gravely and, I think, unfairly. In some biographical commentaries, she's a staid, old-fashioned, people-hating spinster who roamed about the Yorkshire moors alone with her dog, or, alternately, a painfully shy and socially awkward girl-woman who was sick whenever she left home. Elsewhere, she's a stubborn and defiant woman who willingly withheld assorted physical and mental ailments, or an ethereal soul too fragile to endure the real world. Seldom is she kind, and in most, she's a superior intellect, a genius unable or unwilling to participate in 'normal' society. With such eccentric images associated with her, it's no wonder that Emily is still perceived today as 'no normal being'.[3] So why is this the case? How fair and reliable are these narratives? And how does Emily appear from a 21st-century perspective?

This chapter tackles these questions by exploring Emily's portrayal in biographies, considering how she's been constructed and distorted through romanticised eulogies, vilifications and overly elevated interpretations. It's impossible to include reference to *all* Brontë biographies here (both those devoted solely to Emily, as well as those focused on other members of the Brontë family), so consider this an edited snapshot of the more pertinent takes on this apparently 'wild' and 'untameable' woman.[4] To navigate this biographical battlefield, however, we need first to go back to the mid-19th century, and the account of Emily offered by her first biographer and mythographer: Charlotte Brontë.

THROUGH CHARLOTTE'S EYES, DARKLY

Charlotte was extremely influential in constructing 'Emily Brontë'. She produced the notorious 'Biographical Notice of Ellis and Acton Bell' and the 'Editor's Preface' to the 1850 edition of *Wuthering Heights*, and in the same year she wrote an introduction to a selection of further poems by 'Ellis Bell'. Charlotte also fictionalised Emily in *Shirley*, and she informed Elizabeth Gaskell's rather outlandish portrayal of Emily in *The Life of Charlotte Brontë*. Charlotte loved her sister, undoubtedly, and was well placed to represent her sister. But as many biographers and literary critics have shown, she offered a manufactured and contradictory account of Emily that deliberately scrambled fact and fiction to portray the Emily *she* wanted.

The most famous of all Charlotte's illusory sketches is the 'Biographical Notice' of 1850, something she composed shortly after her siblings' deaths, when she was emotionally raw and vulnerable. In it, she declared a need to 'explain briefly the origin and authorship of the books written by Currer, Ellis, and Acton Bell', whose work had been labelled as coarse, brutal and degrading by contemporary critics. She also wanted to correct the misheld assumption that the Bells were one and the same person.[5] Charlotte's aims were admirable, but her portrayal of Emily was somewhat unkind:

> *My sister Emily was not a person of demonstrative character, nor one on the recesses of whose mind and feelings even those nearest and dearest to her could, with impunity, intrude unlicensed [...] In Emily's nature the extremes of vigour and simplicity seemed to meet. Under an unsophisticated culture, inartificial tastes, and an unpretending outside, lay a secret power and fire that might have informed the brain and kindled the veins of a hero; but she had no worldly wisdom; her powers were unadapted to the practical business of life; she would fail to defend her most manifest rights, to consult her most legitimate advantage[.] Her will was not very flexible, and it generally opposed her interest. Her temper was*

magnanimous, but warm and sudden; her spirit alto-
gether unbending.[6]

It's this conception of Emily by Charlotte that has persisted ever since. Here, Emily is conceived of as impenetrable
to her 'nearest and dearest' (ergo, she was stubborn), with an
'unbending spirit' (meaning, she was difficult), and her creative
talents were those of a child-woman (for which read, she was
immature and didn't know what she was doing). To be fair to
Charlotte though, she moderates her words towards the end of
the piece, concluding poignantly that 'for strangers [Emily and
Anne] were nothing, for superficial observers less than nothing; but for those who had known them all their lives in the
intimacy of close relationship, they were genuinely good and
truly great'.[7]

If only she had stopped there, but she didn't. Her Editor's
Preface, which also appeared in the second edition of *Wuthering
Heights*, was even more fallacious. In this commentary, she
ravages Emily's novel:

> *I have just read over Wuthering Heights, and, for the first
> time, have obtained a clear glimpse of what are termed
> (and, perhaps, really are) its faults [.] With regard to the
> rusticity of the [the novel], I admit the charge, for I feel the
> quality. It is moorish, and wild, and knotty as a root of
> heath. Nor was it natural that it should be otherwise; the
> author being herself a native and nursling of the moors.
> Doubtless, had her lot been cast in a town, her writings, if
> she had written at all, would have possessed another char-
> acter[.] Had Ellis Bell been a lady or a gentleman accus-
> tomed to what is called 'the world', her view of a remote
> and unreclaimed region, as well as of the dwellers therein,*

would have differed greatly from that actually taken by the home-bred country girl [.] Where delineation of human character is concerned [,] I am bound to avow that she had scarcely more practical knowledge of the peasantry amongst whom she lived, than a nun has of the country people who sometimes pass her convent gates. My sister's disposition was not naturally gregarious; circumstances favoured and fostered her tendency to seclusion; except to go to church or take a walk on the hills, she rarely crossed the threshold of home. Though her feeling for the people round was benevolent, intercourse with them she never sought; nor, with very few exceptions, ever experienced [...] her mind had gathered of the real concerning them, was too exclusively confined to those tragic and terrible traits of which, in listening to the secret annals of every rude vicarage, the memory is sometimes compelled to repress. Her imagination, which was a spirit more sombre than sunny, more powerful than sportive, found in such traits material whence it wrought creations like Heathcliff, Earnshaw, like Catherine. Having formed these beings, she did not know what she had done [...] Heathcliff, indeed, stands unredeemed; never once swerving in his arrow-straight course to perdition [.] Whether it is right or advisable to create things like Heathcliff, I do not know.[8]

Reading Charlotte's assessment today, the words of her own fiery protagonist, Jane Eyre, come to mind: 'Unjust! Unjust,' cries the young Jane to her tormenter, John Reed.[9] People are often shocked to learn that Charlotte wrote such words about her recently deceased siblings. And it is hard to make a convincing case that she had good intentions, given that Charlotte certainly doesn't pull any punches. The phrase 'nursling of the moors' cruelly infantilises Emily, putting a pejorative spin on her beloved moorland outings. Likewise, the suggestion that her sister was a 'home-bred country girl' is disparaging, reinforcing Emily as unworldly and insular. And although Charlotte pays homage to her sister by acknowledging her as a formidable writer, she undermines this by suggesting that Emily had little power over her violent creativity and produced figures such as Heathcliff in innocence.

Charlotte didn't reserve her scorn just for Emily. Anne was condemned, too. She famously denounced Anne's second novel as 'an entire mistake', and asked their publisher not to re-issue the book during her lifetime.[10] Fortunately, Anne's response to her critics can be found in her own preface to the second edition of *The Tenant of Wildfell Hall* (1848), and her assertions there firmly counter Charlotte's attack, suggesting that the novel was not a 'mistake' at all, but a decidedly political venture.

Charlotte fuelled her conception of Emily by relaying it to Elizabeth Gaskell, who reproduced it in *The Life of Charlotte Brontë*. Like many subsequent biographers, Gaskell never met Emily in person; by the time she made her first visit to the parsonage in 1853, Emily was long dead. But this didn't stop her declaring that, based on what she had heard from Charlotte, she didn't really like Emily: 'all that I, a stranger, have been able to learn about her has not tended to give either me, or my readers, a pleasant impression of her' (while Charlotte was 'genuinely good, and truly great').[11] Gaskell's dislike of Emily is wildly apparent. Consequently, she avers that Emily was

> *...extremely reserved in manner. I distinguish reserve from shyness, because I imagine shyness would please, if it knew how, whereas reserve is indifferent whether it pleases*

or not. Anne, like her eldest sister, was shy; Emily was reserved [...] Emily - that free, wild, untameable spirit, never happy nor well but on the sweeping moors that gathered round her home - that hater of strangers, doomed to live among them, and not merely to live but slave in their service.[12]

Surely, Gaskell could have noted Emily's reserve without further judgment (as Ellen Nussey went on to do)? Instead, she offered a saintly image of Charlotte and misconstrued Emily, using inflammatory language to accentuate Emily as rude, something she labours over by contrasting Charlotte (and Anne's) positive shyness with Emily's stern aloofness. Gaskell also reframed Emily's need for privacy, uses provocative vocabulary to renovate her preference for seclusion to a charge of people-hating.

Today, such personality traits would not be received or relayed with the same misshapen judgment that they were in the mid-19th century. Nowadays, being shy or reserved is recognised as a composite part of some people's personalities, which are multifaceted and complex. And we accept that people display character traits in myriad ways in different situations. In fact, we're more likely to compensate for any awkwardness felt by friends, colleagues or family members in social situations, going out of our way to minimise their anxieties. Privacy and seclusion, too, is seen as a personal choice that's to be respected by others. In fact, to invade another's privacy or push in where one is clearly unwelcome is regarded itself as the problem (Lockwood in *Wuthering Heights* again springs to mind). Perhaps, then, in this respect, Emily would fit in more comfortably in modern society. She would certainly be received less brusquely and her individualism would be less scrutinised.

Significantly, in recent years, some (but not all) Brontë biographers have begun to objectively critique Charlotte's tale of an isolated yet clever family grouping, whose inexperience led them in their ignorance to creativity. Now her tale is recognised as part of her own extraordinary strategy to control the authorial narrative of her sisters and herself (though she didn't account for the inadvertent creation of a Charlotte vs. Emily dichotomy that emerged since the 19th century. Even in my own commentary Charlotte appears villainous – sorry, Charlotte!).

Books like Juliet Barker's authoritative biography, *The Brontës*, and Lucasta Miller's sharply detailed criticism, *The Brontë Myth* (2001), a metabiography that unravels many of the erroneous ideas often attributed to the various Brontës, have proven that Charlotte's narrative was wildly overblown and that Gaskell slipped regularly between fact and fiction, liberally embellishing stories and ideas here and there in order to canonise her favourite author, Charlotte.

Importantly, Emily's biographers, too, have begun to evaluate the mythic images that have so resolutely stuck to her. Not only have they questioned Charlotte's version of her sister, but re-considered the relationship between the sisters, finding that sibling tension may provide a possible motive for Charlotte's account. Edward Chitham, for instance, one of Emily's most respected biographers, has argued that the pair had a turbulent relationship that dated from their teenage years, and he shows how an entry in Branwell's *The History of the Young Men* from 1831 provides evidence of the quarrel between them:

> After an altercation, Parry goes to rest, but Tracky 'came
> up and unceremonisciously sat upon him'. Parry humped
> up and 'stamped upon' his enemy. But the chief genius Talli

(Charlotte) came in and seized him to protect him, 'and the Ch-Gn-Emii took up her favourite Parry. But from this time forward a great hatred has subsisted between the two heroes, and also between Ross, or Trott as the King called him, and his monarch.'[13]

Here, Branwell's account points to power dynamics as the cause of problems between the sisters. Importantly, Chitham acknowledges the speculative nature of his supposition, yet his well-constructed argument offers a fascinating perspective.

Another of Emily's biographers, John Hewish, offers the view that Emily had baffled yet fascinated Charlotte since childhood. Hewish contends that Charlotte could not get a grip of her sister's character because so many of Emily's personality traits were in opposition to her own. Of course, neither of these accounts can ever be proven, but they offer interesting insights and speculative possibilities about the siblings' dynamics.

Sadly, though, what's really important is that the effect of Charlotte's self-fashioned construction of her sister, along with Gaskell's distorted representation, have had a durable and troubling impact on Emily's reputation. In their day, they reduced her almost immediately to cliché and stereotype, and this idea remains prevalent today. In the 19th century, it was another thirty-five years before the first full biography of Emily was published (by Agnes Mary Robinson), giving plenty of time for these erroneous ideas to take hold. And, in the meantime, the biographical shreds offered by Charlotte and Gaskell have enabled all kinds of fanciful new yarns about Emily to be spun.

TO BE FOREVER UNSTABLE

A persistent topic in Brontë biographies and scholarly writing concerns the family's emotional and physical health. In *The Brontës in Context* (2012), Janis McLarren Caldwell's scrutiny of 'mental health' is a good example how such a discussion typically unfolds:

> *We might think of the Brontë sisters as exhibiting rather robust mental health, given that they weathered the loss of so many intimate family members; though grieving normally, they seemingly remained both functional and productive. But Patrick Brontë, and all of his children who survived into adulthood, suffered forms of what we would call neurosis. Each experienced a different kind, attributing his or her distress to one of the multiple types of mental illness described in the Victorian period.*[14]

Here, the tentative phrasing in the first sentence (of the piece) quickly leads on to a harsher diagnosis for 'all' of the Brontë family in the second statement. [15] The chapter in question is fascinating, but sadly, it's also an example of how the Brontë family is often characterised as psychologically abnormal, and Emily, in particular, has been repeatedly read as suffering from varied ailments. The account of her 'neurosis' offered by McLarren Caldwell focuses on her well-being away from home and is also common in Brontë biographies: 'Under the stress of leaving home for school at Roe Head, Emily experienced a homesickness expressed as wasting and weakness.'[16] Indeed, Emily's departure from Roe Head is often the basis for her subsequent diagnosed with numerous medical ills. But is the case as straightforward as has been suggested?

The origins of the story can (again) be traced to Charlotte who, as we've already seen, was somewhat prone to exaggeration (and outright falsification) when it came to Emily. She provided Gaskell with an account of her sister's ill health as a teenager. Emily left Miss Wooler's Roe Head school in October 1835, having arrived there just three months earlier because, as Charlotte declares, a debilitating form of homesickness made her physically and mentally ill:

> *Liberty was the breath of Emily's nostrils; without it she perished. The change from her own home to a school, and from her very own noiseless, very secluded, but unrestricted and unartificial mode of life, to one of disciplined routine (though under the kindest auspices), was what she failed in enduring. Her nature proved here too strong for her fortitude [...] Nobody knew what ailed her but me. I knew only too well. In this struggle her health was quickly broken: her white face, attenuated form, and failing strength, threatened rapid decline. I felt in my heart she would die, if she did not go home, and with this conviction obtained her recall.*[17]

Charlotte's account is filled with sorrow and concern, but she also accentuates the forcible symptoms that necessitated Emily's immediate return home, which happened without delay. Here, again, Charlotte reinforces herself as a moral, motherly heroine in Emily's life, making herself sympathetic to Gaskell. But if, as we've seen, Charlotte was a slippery witness when it came to Emily, just how accurate is she here?

In *The Brontë Myth*, Lucasta Miller challenges notions of psychological abnormality attributed to the Brontës. Of the anecdote in question, Miller notes how, in 'Charlotte's version of events, it is she, not Emily herself, who realises that her sister must go home. Emily is passive, and Charlotte the protector who stirs herself to action just in time to prevent catastrophe'.[18] That Emily was unhappy and her unhappiness manifest physically is not in question; after all, it is a documented fact that she returned home to the parsonage so soon after departing. But Charlotte implicitly diagnoses Emily with homesickness here, glossing over the complex circumstances that might nuance this assessment.

Not only was this Emily's first time away from home in several years, a place that had been a place of safety and freedom to her, but it was also her first experience away from home since her brief period at the Clergy Daughters' School in Cowan Bridge ten years earlier where her sisters had become gravely ill. And we know, of course, that Emily was a homebody: she loved being in Haworth, as the lines of 'A little while, a little while', cited earlier, indicate. It's also likely that Charlotte slept in her own room away from the dormitory where Emily was based, so Emily may have felt ill at ease or lonely in her newfound residential circumstances. Likewise, at Roe Head, Emily was disadvantaged in ways that Charlotte was not: she had limited educational experience beyond the home and yet she was clever beyond her years. She was also the oldest and possibly tallest pupil at the school, so was physically out of sync with her peers. Her relationship to her teacher 'may have made her vulnerable to unpleasantness from, or even ostracism by, her fellow pupils'.[19] And the school routine left little time for private conversation, or creative writing.

Together, these circumstances provide a more nuanced understanding of Emily's unhappiness, clarifying why she may have been so physically and emotionally upset as to want to leave. To me, three months seems a reasonable period for someone to try out a new situation, give it a fair go, and decide if it is for them or not. But history has not been this generous to Emily and these circumstances are often glossed over and simply categorised as 'neurosis'.

Significantly, on this point too, Emily's biographers have offered alternative explanations for her rapid departure from Roe Head. Robert Barnard, for instance, accepts the 'essential truth' of Charlotte's statement, but also wonders 'whether other facts were involved', speculating that the seventeen-year-old Emily found the teaching at Roe Head somewhat 'childish and unstimulating', especially given how clever she was.[20] Barnard also points out that 'this is something Charlotte would not have stressed, for fear of offending Miss Wooler' (more so because a later teacher noted that Emily was also superior to Charlotte in this respect).[21]

John Hewish, however, believes that Charlotte manipulated the evidence and presented Emily as frail and sick to suit her own story, in which she cast herself as a protective and motherly elder sister. For Hewish, Emily had toughness of mind and she probably just disliked the new life routines and preferred to return home. After all, this was a woman who had not had to endure daily structure for the majority of her formative years. Hewish also draws on Emily's writing to explain how Charlotte may have reached her interpretation, noting that in *Wuthering Heights* Emily provides insight into the challenge of adjustment, when Catherine Earnshaw tells Nelly of her grief from separating from Heathcliff:

> *I cannot say why I felt so wildly wretched: it must have been temporary derangement for there is scarcely cause. But, supposing at twelve years old, I had been wrenched from the Heights, and every early association, and my all*

*in all, as Heathcliff was at that time, and been converted at
a stroke into Mrs Linton, the lady of Thrushcross Grange,
and the wife of a stranger: an exile, and outcast, thence-
forth, from what had been my world. You may fancy a
glimpse of the abyss where I grovelled! [...] Oh, I'm burn-
ing! I wish I were out of doors! I wish I were a girl again,
half savage and hardy, and free; and laughing at injuries,
not maddening under them! Why am I so changed? why
does my blood rush into a hell of tumult at a few words?
I'm sure I should be myself were I once among the heather
on those hills.*[22]

Nonetheless, Charlotte's focus on Emily's apparent anxiety
away from home (especially in her teenage years) raised a
question mark over Emily's emotional stability that's paved
the way for the many psycho-biographical interpretations that
have followed. It's understandable that a sensationalised image
presents rich pickings for a biographer. After all, they are in the
business of writing and selling books and today, in our culture
of 'spin', sensationalism more than ever is (sadly) deemed a
marketing plus.

Yet this can also be problematic, especially in the case of
Emily Brontë. Emily's own autobiographical silence, coupled
with the many questionable second-hand accounts of her,
leave a gap in our understanding of her that's made her ripe for
posthumous diagnosis with emotional ailments. And perhaps
this was inevitable anyway, given that her only novel features
ill health and neurotic ways of being so prominently. But such
readings of Emily still dominate her legacy and recently they've
been expanded. Indeed, in the most recent and speculative
commentaries, Emily has been associated with three particular
medical conditions that feature prominently in 21st-century

psychology and science: agoraphobia, anorexia and Asperger's syndrome.

The idea that Emily was agoraphobic, an anxiety disorder that gravitates around a fear of public spaces and often finds expression in subjects not wanting to leave their home, stems from comments on Emily's extreme reserve coupled with Charlotte's observation that Emily was 'something of a recluse' and the stories of Emily's homesickness. Dana Stevens has flippantly commented that 'Emily's reclusiveness bordered on agoraphobia', while Maureen Adams has stated that today, Emily 'might be classified as an avoidant personality disorder or an agoraphobic'.[23] Dolores Malet, meanwhile, wonders how Emily's 'reclusive, agoraphobic nature' led to the creation of a novel like *Wuthering Heights*.[24]

Elizabeth Gaskell, whose account of Emily in The Life of Charlotte Brontë (1857) – informed by Charlotte's descriptions – is responsible for much of the 'mad Emily' mythology.

To me, the development from 'recluse' to agoraphobic is an overstatement. There's no evidence that Emily experienced any of the other symptoms that usually manifest in agoraphobia, such as panic attacks, sweating, sticky palms and hyperventilating, and we also know she did successfully leave home on several occasions, such as travelling with Charlotte to Belgium. So to couple Emily's reserve and preference for solitude as evidence of agoraphobia is fairly misleading to me and imposes a limit on the ways in which we might otherwise understand her personality and love of home.

The claim that Emily was anorexic is made by Katherine Frank in *Emily Brontë: A Chainless Soul* (1990). I am a huge admirer of Frank's biography. The image of Emily she offers readily chimes with my own imaginary, particularly Frank's emphasis on Emily's refusal of victimhood. But I depart from Frank on one major assertion:

> *If Emily Brontë were alive today and could be prevailed upon to submit to psychiatric treatment (a most unlikely prospect), she would most certainly be diagnosed as suffering from anorexia nervosa. Not merely her refusal to eat and her extreme slenderness and preoccupation with food and cooking, but also her obsessive need for control, her retreat into an ongoing, interior fantasy world, and her social isolation are all characteristic of the 'anorectic personality' described by psychiatrists [and] feminist writers.*[25]

Frank says she's 'less interested in retroactive medical diagnosis' than in 'what must have been the experience' of Emily's 'illness'. But she *does* retrospectively diagnose Emily, asking how she felt 'to be perpetually hungry and to deny that hunger'.[26] The leading question embeds *her* assumption that Emily *was* anorexic and it is followed later by an imaginary commentary in Emily's mind: 'I hate it here. I will not eat. I want to go home. I refuse to grow up, to grow big. I will make myself ill, starve even, unless I am released', she has Emily saying.[27] And, as evidence for her medical claim, Frank avers that

> *As a Victorian woman, as the unendowered daughter of an obscure clergyman, Emily Brontë possessed scant power or control over the world she inhabited or over the course of her own life. She responded to her helplessness in two ways, both of which granted the illusion of power: through anorexic behaviour and writing.*[28]

The idea that Emily lacked control of her life conflicts with other accounts of her, not least Charlotte's perception of Emily's stubbornness (which doesn't suggest a lack of control at all). Certainly, in the patriarchal context of her time, Emily lacked overt social power, but she also assumed control of her life in many ways.

As we've seen, there's evidence to suggest that she proactively turned from periods of education and employment when they didn't suit her; she explored the potential opening of a school with her sisters and travelled to Belgium to upskill in languages and music; *she* made the decision to stay at home and govern the parsonage's domestics of her own volition (having inherited monies from Aunt Branwell); and, of course, she gave consent to Charlotte's publishing vision, writing a book of extraordinary power that moved the literary circles of its day. In this context, it feels like Emily had significant control of her life. So, for me, to identify Emily's occasional disordered eating is one thing – especially when it's based on Charlotte's evidence and occurred during times of sickness (because who doesn't stop eating when they're feeling unwell?) – but to diagnose Emily as anorexic, based on an imaginary interior dialogue, is quite another.

Finally, the recent suggestion that Emily experienced Asperger's syndrome derives from off-the-cuff comments that Claire Harman made in the promotion of her 2015 biography, *Charlotte Brontë: A Life.*[29] At the Edinburgh International Book Festival in 2016 Harman casually remarked that

> *I think Charlotte and everybody was quite frightened of Emily. I think she was an Asperger's-ey person [.] She was such a genius and had total imaginative freedom [...] Containing Emily, protecting Emily, not being alarmed by Emily, was a big project for the whole household. She's an absolutely fascinating person – a very troubling presence, though.*[30]

The media responded to Harman's lurid suggestions with uninhibited speculation: 'Emily Brontë may have had Asperger syndrome, according to the literary biographer Claire Harman', wrote *The Guardian.*[31] Harman's conclusion is based on the idea that Emily 'hated' to leave home, she punched her dog in the face (said Gaskell, I'll come back to this in Chapter Four!), came from an 'unusual' family, and her father was also 'a bit Asperger's-ey too'.[32] Again we see how because Emily (apparently) exhibited *some* behaviours associated with autism, this is uncritically accepted as evidence and repackaged for speculative diagnosis. Writing in frustration at Harman's comments, Emily Willingham reflects on this 'freewheeling approach to characterising what it means to be on the autistic spectrum'.[33] Willingham views it as an irresponsible and 'casual way to apply a disability label, a usage that people seem to think is OK with mental or developmental disabilities when they'd never apply it with physical disabilities. People don't ever seem to say, "He's a little paraplegic-ey.'"[34]

Like Gaskell's biography, Harman's book isn't especially sympathetic to Emily. We know that Emily suffered sometimes in different forms when she left home (as many would have given the circumstance). We know that she was intense and preferred solitude. We also know that she had a special bond with her many pets (as I look at in Chapter Four). But as Willingham points out,

> People seem to think that the sole features of autism involve being solitary and odd, possibly with a dash of 'magic disabled supergenius' thrown in and a prickly temperament. Of course, those traits also fit people who are antisocial, or have some form of schizophrenia, bipolar disorder, some other personality disorder, a history of abuse and loss, unmatched talent or nothing at all.[35]

To diagnose Emily with austism, anorexia or Asperger's when it relies on casual observation and unreliable information, then, is nearly impossible, especially when the information we have about Emily is *so* sparse. Clearly, there's a passion motivating those who want to understand her better, but it's ill-advised to scrawl over the limited information available about Emily and reach spurious conclusions about her health, 'Like Asperger's-y', as Willingham observes. [36]

EMILY: FRIEND, FRIENDLY OR FOE?

As a final word on the biographical portrayals of Emily, I want to briefly consider her time in Belgium. At the end of

Emily's beloved pets and 'special friends': Keeper, her bullmastiff;
Flossy, Anne's dog; and Tiger, the family cat.

her first six months there, she began to teach music at the
Pensionnat Héger. Her first pupils were three English girls,
the Wheelwright sisters. While they found Charlotte kind and
friendly and invited her to their home, they felt differently
about Emily. Laetitia, the girls' elder sister, 'disliked her from
the first', adding:

> She taught my three youngest sisters music for four months,
> much to my annoyance, as she would only take them in
> their play hours, so as not to curtail her own school hours,
> naturally causing many tears to small children, the eldest
> ten, the youngest not seven.[37]

Laetitia's stern view of Emily has clearly been influenced by
the inconvenience to her and her sisters' leisure time. However,
it has been read as evidence of Emily's 'self-centredness which

allowed her to ride rough-shod over her young pupils' feelings'.[38] Laetitia's account is righteously biased (who wants to have their social time taken up by enforced study?), but surely Emily should be treated a bit more fairly for the scheduling of her tutorials? It seems perfectly reasonable to me anyhow, and doesn't amount to 'rough-shodding' anyone's feelings.

But another factor to note here is that the Wheelwrights also disliked Emily more broadly. They loved Charlotte and regularly invited her to socialise, but they begrudged Emily's presence and would tease her about her (lack of) dress sense. They made fun of Emily's hand-sewn clothes that had old-fashioned puffy sleeves and laughed at how her skirt hung strangely around her legs (her exceptionally long legs) because she refused to wear petticoats. Charlotte, we know, happily conformed to modern ways of dress, 'learning from the Belgian girls to wear embroidered collars and tailor her dresses to flatter her small frame', but Emily wouldn't conform, and resisted their peer pressure, quipping bluntly that she wished 'to be as God made me'.[39] Often these words are repeated as evidence of Emily's harsh, stern manner, but reading it now it seems somewhat comical, as if Emily was nipping the Wheelwrights' petty observations rather firmly in the bud with a conversation-stopper. I'm pretty confident she would have known this would stop them in their tracks. Besides which, today she'd be the height of fashion in the catch-all for older styles and quirky dress: vintage.

But, irrespective of these accounts of Emily's 'anti-social' behaviour, they are countered and balanced by reports of her friendship with another pupil, sixteen-year-old Louise de Bassompierre. Louise preferred Emily to Charlotte, finding her 'more sympathetic, kinder and more approachable'.[40] And Emily seems to have responded with friendship and kindness, giving Louise a pencil drawing of a weather-torn pine tree that she had produced which, it's said, Louise treasured ever after. Perhaps, then, Louise, like Ellen Nussey, encountered a different Emily, the one that Emily's biographer, Winifred Gérin, reports to be 'vivacious in conversation' and who enjoyed 'giving pleasure'.[41] Perhaps, too, Emily saw in Louise something of her sister Anne, whom she loved and looked out for (as reports of her comforting Anne during her asthma attacks indicate).

If Emily wasn't 'all bad', then, one other voice from Belgium affirms this: Constantin Héger, Charlotte and Emily's tutor. Héger got to know each Brontë sibling from their time at the Pensionnat Héger, and he provided some interesting comments on the pair. He noted, for instance, that Emily seemed to exercise a sort of tyranny on Charlotte, something that's been interpreted to mean that Charlotte always seemed to appease Emily. But he also praised Emily to Gaskell, which is rather surprising since Charlotte suggested that Héger and Emily didn't really get on. Héger did not remember an 'ignorant' or 'timed' girl who 'featured in his school reports', but instead recalled 'an extraordinary young woman' whose

> *Powerful reason would have deduced new spheres of discovery from the knowledge of the old; and her strong, imperious will would never have been daunted by opposition or difficulty; never have given way but with life....her faculty of imagination was such that, if she had written a history, her view of scenes and characters would have been so vivid, and so powerfully expressed, and supported by such a show of argument, that it would have dominated over the reader, whatever might have been his previous opinions, or his cooler perceptions of its truth.* [42]

Sometimes Héger's words, especially his reference to Emily's 'imperious will', have been used to reinforce readings of Emily as forceful, dominant and dogmatic. Certainly, such vocabulary is open to this suggestion. But I think that, coming from a rather patriarchal figure in the mid-19th century, Héger's words are actually positive. He recognises Emily's individuality and praises her for it. He notes her sense of agency, her strong, thoughtful mind and creative imagination, and casts them positively. It leaves me with the sense that he was suitably impressed by the young Brontë. For me, together with stories by Louise and, of course, Ellen Nussey, we see glimpses of Emily's personality and they give us a sense that Emily had a human side to her 'genius', too.

THREE

ELLIS BELL

A reproduction of the profile portrait of Emily painted
c. 1833–34 by Branwell, as part of a group painting.

Writing was not simply a genteel pastime for Emily Brontë – it was a way of life, which she took very seriously. In 1846, she adopted the pseudonym 'Ellis Bell' for the publication of the sisters' poems, for which they paid £36 to publishers Aylott and Jones for the privilege.

Despite the sisters' popularity today, *Poems by Currer, Ellis and Acton Bell* was not a commercial success. However, the early reviews were reasonable. Of them, the *Critic* bestowed high praise on the collection, declaring it 'good, wholesome, refreshing, vigorous poetry' with 'no sickly affectations', 'no tedious imitations' and 'no namby-pamby'.[1] Instead, the anonymous critic stated, 'original thoughts are expressed in the true language of poetry'.[2]

Emily's poems were singled out, too. 'Ellis Bell' is an 'inspiration', declared the reviewer in *Athenaeum*, with an 'an evident power of wing', whose work 'may yet find an audience in the outer world'.[3] Today, Emily's recognised as one of the great English lyric poets, finding admirers among other writers. In 1877, Algernon Charles Swinburne described her as a 'passionate great genius', and Peter Bayne, writing in 1881, stated that 'the poems of Emily Brontë excel those of her sisters' because 'they are superior in occasional splendour' and 'serene intensity'.[4] The Victorian poet Emily Dickinson, meanwhile, thought Emily 'gigantic'.[5] She was so passionate about Emily's poems that she chose 'No coward soul' to be read at her funeral. Virginia Woolf even suggested that Emily's poems may outlast the legacy of *Wuthering Heights*.

With such high literary praise, it's worth revisiting the story behind Emily's authorial transition to 'Ellis Bell', and thinking about just what the special 'something' is that has made her poems so arresting for readers across the years. Perhaps we will discover new reasons for why audiences today might want to read them, and why, as Swinburne put it, she was 'a poetess for the next generation'.[6]

EMILY'S 'RHYMES'

The story behind the publication of Emily's poems (or 'rhymes', as she called them) is a fascinating one. In 1844, she began copying her poems into two notebooks. There's the notebook titled *Gondal Poems* in which she copied some of her writings from when she was younger, and a second text that was untitled, but is known today as the 'Honresfeld manuscript'. We don't know why Emily separated her poems. Perhaps she had thoughts of publishing the material, or maybe Emily just thought that her best poems read better without reference to Gondal.[7] Either way, in autumn 1845, Charlotte discovered the books in Emily's portable writing desk. The poems stirred her immediately, as her account of the literary discovery reveals:

> *One day, in the autumn of 1845, I accidentally lighted on a MS. Volume of verse in my sister Emily's handwriting. Of course, I was not surprised, knowing that she could and did write verse. I looked it over, and something more than surprise seized me, – a deep conviction that these were not common effusions, not at all like the poetry women generally write. I thought them condensed and terse, vigorous and genuine. To my ear, they had also had a peculiar music – wild, melancholy, elevating.*[8]

The discovery made a huge impact on Charlotte and she was convinced that the poems warranted publication. Back in 1836, she had written to Robert Southey, the Poet Laureate, expressing her dreams for literary renown, and he had 'mansplained' back to her about women's proper place. Finding Emily's poems, however, reignited Charlotte's literary dreams, and she propositioned her sister with the idea.

But Emily was less than impressed. She was furious at the intrusion on her privacy. She had been a secret poet, and producing verse was a personal and intimate experience for her. Even Anne, who shared the world of Gondal with Emily, didn't know the complete content of her sister's poetic oeuvre. She reveals an awareness of the poems in her Diary Papers, but she didn't approach her sister about the specifics. Perhaps that's why, by 1845, she had become disillusioned with Gondal.

A page from the Diary Papers.

Anyhow, with Charlotte snooping through her belongings, Emily was fuming. It wasn't just that her privacy had been violated, or that her poetic world invaded, though; it was Charlotte's suggestion that the material should be published that was 'an unforgivable offence'.[9] Charlotte later reported how 'it took hours to reconcile her to the discovery I had made, and days to persuade her that such poems merited publication'.[10] Thankfully, Charlotte persisted: 'I knew, however, that a mind like hers could not be without some latent spark of honourable ambition, and refused to be discouraged in my attempts to fan that spark to flame.'[11]

Eventually, Emily was persuaded by her sister to pursue publication, and this was helped by the fact that Anne had offered some poems for publication in the collection, too. But unlike the arresting impact of Emily's verse, Charlotte wasn't overly enthused by Anne's compositions, merely noting that they had a 'sweet sincere pathos' of their own.[12] But if they were going to publish, there were some conditions to be met: the Gondal origins of the verse would be disguised by careful editing of the text, the poems *had* to be published under a pseudonym, and the sisters' true identities needed to remain a secret. With an agreement reached, the sisters formally commenced their literary careers.

Between September and early January 1846 Emily began selecting the material she wished to include in the collection as well as the process of 'de-Gondaling' it. The edits she made have been the subject of much scrutiny and debate, and some of the changes she made are fascinating. The bleak ending of 'Cold in the earth', for instance, which had previously read 'Severed at last by Time's all-severing wave', was streamlined, appearing in the final manuscript with the repetition removed, creating the more elegant 'Severed at last by Time's all wearing wave'.[13] From this we can see that Emily didn't just develop her prose; she undertook a line-by-line, word-by-word sweep of her material, polishing everything.

While Emily was busy at work on her poems, Charlotte set about finding a publisher. Later, she articulated the reasoning behind the sisters' *noms de plume*, which revealed an astute insight into the mid-Victorian literary marketplace:

> *Averse to personal publicity, we veiled our own names under those of Currer, Ellis, and Acton Bell; the ambiguous choice being dictated by a sort of conscientious scruple at assuming Christian names positively masculine, while we did not like to declare ourselves women, because – without at that time suspecting that our mode of writing and thinking was not what is called 'feminine' – we had a vague impression that authoresses are liable to be looked on with prejudice; we had noticed how critics sometimes use for their chastisement the weapon of personality, and for their reward, a flattery, which is not true praise.*[14]

The sisters, then, were aware of the challenges they would face as women participating in the male-dominated literary world, and clearly understood that a sexual double standard pervaded the industry. Realising that it would be difficult to publish as women and knowing that their work would be unfairly prejudged, the Brontës joined the many other women writers, such as Mary Ann Evans (better known as George Eliot), who published under authorial disguise. Charlotte, Emily and Anne didn't just pick straightforward 'men's' names for their project, though. They deliberately chose ambiguous, gender-neutral ones: Currer, Ellis and Acton.

Poems comprised twenty-one pieces by both Emily and Anne, and nineteen by Charlotte. But her poems are far longer than those by her siblings, occupying more than half of the volume. After Emily's death, Charlotte alighted on more poems by Emily and Anne, and in the 'prefatory note' to *Selections from Poems by Ellis Bell* (1850), she suggested that 'It would not have been difficult to compile a volume out of the papers left by my sisters'.[15] Although this never happened, today there's approximately 200 known poems and fragments of poetry by Emily in existence, of which 168 are available are now available in manuscript form and have been published in standalone collections. It's through this work that we get a tantalising glimpse of Emily's imagination.

GONDAL

In their Diary Paper of summer 1837, Emily drew herself and Anne writing at their dining table. Emily is sat with her back to us and Anne sits opposite her. There are papers sprawled across the table and the sisters appear hard at work. Anne asks, 'well do you intend to write in the evening', to which Emily responds, 'well what you think'.[16] This is followed by a comment in brackets that states 'we agree to go out 1st to make sure if we Get into a humor we may stay'.[17] Poor spelling and punctuation aside, the conversation between the sisters is enlightening. Anne's question isn't really a question since she knows full well that Emily will want to write all evening, and Emily's retort is somewhat rhetorical, as the digression in brackets implies. The piece captures the sisters' literary partnership, and their attitudes to the Gondal poems. Emily, unlike Anne, never left this creative world.

Indeed, many of Emily's published works originate from the imaginary world of Gondal, which was a huge, sprawling fantasy saga fuelled by salacious tales of love, imprisonment, murder, drama and intrigue (think *Game of Thrones*, but run by women). But what's frustrating for any Emily fan is that no complete prose description of the epic survives, so Emily's (and Anne's) pre-annotated poems provide the only clue to the complete picture of the fantasy saga.

In the 'Gondal notebook', Emily unfolds the prose poems chronologically, but the pieces are also often grouped according to character. In another book, however, *A Grammar of General Geography for the Use of Schools and Young Persons*, she copied a list of Gondal place names.[18] Under the heading 'A vocabulary of proper names…to be committed to memory', Emily pencilled the following details:

> *Alexandia, A kingdom in Gaaldine*
> *Almedore, a kingdom in Gaaldine*
> *Elseraden, a kingdom in Gaaldine*
> *Galladine, a large island newly discovered in the South Pacific*
> *Gondal, a large island in the North Pacific*
> *Regina, the capital of Gondal*
> *Ula, a kingdom in Gaaldine, governed by 4 Sovereigns*
> *Zelona, a kingdom in Gaaldine*
> *Zedora, a large Province in Gaaldine, Governed by a Viceroy.*[19]

There are echoes of Angria in the description presented here, but equally, for a modern-day reader, the material evokes many of the iconic science fiction sagas that today are so admired in popular culture, such as *Star Wars*, *Star Trek* or, even, the *Lord of the Rings* trilogy. Indeed, because the fragment is so tantalisingly suggestive, with its well-planned landscape and detailed place names, it's easy to imagine the narrative being adapted into a popular film series in its own right, with each kingdom forming a spin-off franchise accompanied by video games and a thriving world of 'fan fiction' to boot.

From the Diary Papers, we also know that Emily and Anne wrote multiple prose narratives that formed the backstory to the poems. So, for instance, in the paper of June 1837, Emily worked on the '1st vol' of Augustus Almedas's life. [20] In July 1841, Anne wrote the '4th volume of Sofala Vernon's life'.[21] By July 1845, the pair were writing the 'Gondal Chronicles', with Emily producing the history of Gondal's 'First Wars', which presumably included 'The Emperor Julius's Life', and Anne composing 'a book by Henry Sophona'.[22]

The Diary Papers also reveal how the sisters transposed aspects from their earlier writings to Gondal. As in the Islanders play, Gondal includes a dreaded Palace of Instruction, where prisoners are besieged into dark, vaulted dungeons with ominous armed guards.[23] In the earlier incarnation in Angria, Emily had been the keeper of the key to the cells for 'naughty school children':

> these cells are dark, vaulted, arched and so far down in the earth that the loudest shriek could not be heard by any inhabitant of the upper world, and in these, as well as the dungeons, the most unjust torturing might go on without any fear of detection.[24]

It's through these imaginary worlds that Emily cultivated her love of the Gothic, and the saga anticipates much of the violence that permeates *Wuthering Heights*. The sisters clearly invested heavily in their fantasy world and Emily, in particular, thrived in the creative process, reporting in her last Diary Paper that the pair 'intend sticking firm by the rascals as long as they delight us which I am glad to say they do'.[25]

While we don't have the complete Gondal saga, Fannie Ratchford did attempt to reconstruct Gondal from the surviving poetry and diary fragments. *Gondal's Queen: A Novel in Verse* (1955) thus recounts the life story of A.G.A. – Emily's shorthand for her heroine, Augusta Geraldine Almeida – tracing her tempestuous life from birth to her death (or murder, as it actually is). This is a fairly old source now and has had many critics, not least because Ratchford presumes that the fragments tell a singular, coherent story and takes licence with some of Emily's characters, mixing them together to make a lone narrative tale. But nonetheless, *Gondal's Queen* remains the first and most comprehensive attempt to reconstruct a fluid Gondal narrative based on Emily's poems. So what does Ratchford find?

Using Emily's list of place names as a point of departure, Ratchford recreates A.G.A.'s life and world. Like Emily, we learn that she is deeply attached to nature, as the poem, 'To the Blue Bell', written in May 1839, indicates:

> *Sacred watcher, wave thy bells!*
> *Fair hill flowers and woodland child!*
> *Dear to me in deep green dells —*
> *Dearest on the mountains wild —*
>
> *Bluebell, even as all divine*
> *I have seen my darling shine —*
> *Bluebell, even as wan and frail*
> *I have seen my darling fail —*
> *Lift thy head and speak to me,*
> *Thou hast found a voice for me —*
> *And soothing words are breathed by thee —*
>
> *Thus they murmur, 'Summer's sun*
> *Warms me till my life is done —*

Would I rather choose to die
Under winter's ruthless sky?

'Glad I bloom, and calm I fade
Weeping twilight dews my bed
Mourner, mourner, dry thy tears,
Sorrow comes with lengthened years.' [26]

But A.G.A.'s relationship with nature isn't the main focus of the story. No, it's the sensationalism of A.G.A.'s turbulent love life that's of more interest to Ratchford. Despite her creative licence, Ratchford shows A.G.A. to be Emily's Byronic heroine, a passionate beauty, who is utterly ruthless in personal and political affairs.

According to Ratchford, then, A.G.A. was 'worshipped by all men who came under her charms', but brought 'tragedy to those upon whom her amorous light shone'.[27] In other words, when she tires of men she disposes of them in one way or another. Her first husband, Lord Alexander, dies violently after being wounded in battle, but A.G.A. does not spend long grieving him: she quickly marries Lord Alfred Sidonia of Aspin Castle, a widower with a child. But she quickly abandons him too for Julius Brenzaida, the Prince of Angora, while poor Alfred is left to die of a broken heart. Julius is, it's said, the love of A.G.A.'s life, but he invades Gondal, believing himself a claimant to the throne. He's quickly assassinated, though, by Angelica, A.G.A.'s onetime stepdaughter, and A.G.A. becomes a fugitive. In time, however, A.G.A. rallies her forces and regains her throne. However, in her loneliness, she meets Fernando and falls in love, but he meets a similar fate to his predecessors: A.G.A. imprisons him and then sends him into exile, where he commits suicide. Finally, A.G.A. is murdered by the outlaw

Douglas at the insistence of Angelica, her former love rival, on Elmor Hill, and only the faithful Lord Eldred, Captain of the Queen's Guards, laments her death.

Ratchford's account is intriguing, especially since the fruit of her labours – a novel in verse – was born from years of detailed research on different manuscripts. But the conflation of several women in Emily's poems – Geraldine, Rosina and Alcona, among others – is problematic because it imposes a limit on our reading of Emily's poems and, importantly, Emily's portrayal of women. Indeed, in Gondal, women are not merely pretty playthings or beautiful trophies to adorn the arms of men; they are strong, determined, fierce, resilient and ambitious, and they are in charge, dictating everything from political agendas and military battles to affairs of the heart. Several critics and biographers have noted that Emily's interest with female authority seems to have come from her fascination with Queen Victoria, who was only ten months younger than her. Emily noted the young Princess's ascension to the throne in her Diary Paper of June 1837 where the reference is interspersed among accounts of Gondal and Angria:

> the Emperors and Empresses of Gondal and Gaaldine pre-
> paring to depart from Gaaldine to Gondal to prepare for
> the coronation which will be on the 12th of July Queen
> Victoria ascended the throne this month. Northangerland
> in Monceys Isle – Zamorna at Eversham.[28]

Clearly, Emily was interested in the Princess' journey and it found expression in Gondal. Moreover, as Brontë scholars such as Christine Alexander have noted, it's this gendered aspect of the tale that sets 'it apart from the male-dominated power structure of Glass Town'.[29]

Ellis Bell

EMILY WRITING LOVE

It's so tempting to read Emily through her published work, especially her poetry, and try to make sense of who she was this way. But it doesn't always pan out because the dramatic events depicted in Gondal – especially its dungeons and prisons – were far removed from her day-to-day life in Haworth (although Gaskell tried to argue that the parsonage was something of a prison). The famous author Muriel Spark, who has also written extensively on Emily, reminds us that

> *No poem by Emily Brontë can possibly tell us whether in 1836 she was unhappy; in 1838, bitter; in 1840, transported with mystic joy. We cannot tell the date on which these emotions stirred within her; we only know the month and year on which her poems were completed (for she has recorded the dates); from this we can tell only that on those particular dates […] she was absorbed in writing a poem about despair or rapture.*[30]

Here, Spark speaks of the danger of reading Emily's poems autobiographically, but she alerts us to something else, namely, the powerful emotional resonance of Emily's writing. And while this doesn't tell us exactly what Emily felt on any given date, it does provide insight into her interests and the philosophical workings of her mind.

One topic that consistently finds expression in Emily's writings is love. Emily never experienced romantic love, but she was exceptionally good at portraying passion in her work. While the absence of any real lover in her life hasn't stopped fans from trying to find a love interest for Emily (see Chapter Seven for more on the wild and often random speculations offered on this subject), we know that she witnessed the prospect of love via her nearest and dearest.

William Weightman, Patrick Brontë's curate, is 'something of a legend in the Brontë story' for this precise reason.[31] Weightman was a frequent visitor to the parsonage and he made friends of all the Brontës, but also seems to have provoked romantic feelings among the sisters – with the exception of Emily, that is. Weightman is most closely associated with Anne, who was said to be in love with him specifically because of her poem 'I will not mourn thee, lovely one' (1842), which was written in the aftermath of his early death. But Juliet Barker has also speculated that Charlotte was infatuated with Weightman, too. And, to be fair, it's not surprising. Weightman was said to be exceedingly handsome (and Charlotte drew his portrait), but he toyed affectionately with the sisters' attentions, playfully sending them all Valentine's cards, for instance, in February 1840 after finding out that they had never received one between them. Emily, it seems, was the only woman in the house unaffected by Weightman's presence, but at least she got to see what infatuation looked like first-hand.

Alongside the family fondness for Weightman, Emily also witnessed the destructive nature of love through Charlotte's seemingly obsessive devotion to her married tutor, Constantin Héger. After she left Brussels in 1844, Charlotte wrote to Héger every fortnight until his wife insisted that she limit her letters to one every six months. The precise nature of their relationship is unclear, but Charlotte's letters – written in French, presumably because, as many biographers have speculated, it loosened the modesty that in English may have constrained Charlotte from declaring her feelings for a married man – fervently express deep admiration for her tutor.

Aptly, unfulfilled and/or tormented love is given prominence in Emily's work, especially, of course, in *Wuthering Heights*, where Heathcliff's love for Catherine Earnshaw is all encompassing and enduring, transcending life and death. But he is also a lover whose passion is destructive, leading him to mourn for the remainder of his life and seek revenge on those who have thwarted him. But Heathcliff is not alone in his inability to recover from the loss of a loved one. Hindley struggles to recover from the death of his wife, Frances, giving in to 'reckless dissipation' to numb his pain.[32] Likewise, Edgar Linton too mourns Catherine, finding consolation through his daughter, Cathy.

Such images of love and loss find expression in Emily's poetry. Indeed, Emily seemed to write quite an extensive amount of break-up poems. [33] There are so many of them that it's easy to imagine a handy travel-sized companion being sold in bookshops. Indeed, 'Emily Brontë's guide to the aftermath of a break-up' could easily be a counter to Valentine's Day woes. Importantly, though, as Laura Inman has noted in her discussion of Emily's prolific break-up outputs, her lovers also often part because of untimely death.[34] So it's quite a morbid take on love (depending on how you see it). The connection between love and death, Inman notes, seems important for Emily, for she often suggests that death, 'even though it severs the relationship, creates an even greater appreciation of, or attachment to, the deceased'.[35] Such an image, of course, is the basis of *Wuthering Heights*, but its origins lie in her poetry. 'Remembrance' (1846), for instance, provides one such example. It anticipates the attitude of Edgar and Heathcliff to Catherine years after her death, but it is actually a Gondal poem, spoken by Rosina Alcona to Julius Brenzaida:

Cold in the earth – and the deep snow piled above thee,
Far, far, removed, cold in the dreary grave!
Have I forgot, my only Love, to love thee,
Severed at last by Time's all-severing wave?

Now, when alone, do my thoughts no longer hover
Over the mountains, on that northern shore,
Resting their wings where heath and fern-leaves cover
Thy noble heart forever, ever more?

Cold in the earth – and fifteen wild Decembers,
From those brown hills, have melted into spring:
Faithful, indeed, is the spirit that remembers
After such years of change and suffering!

Sweet Love of youth, forgive, if I forget thee,
While the world's tide is bearing me along;
Other desires and other hopes beset me,
Hopes which obscure, but cannot do thee wrong!

No later light has lightened up my heaven,
No second morn has ever shone for me;
All my life's bliss from thy dear life was given,
All my life's bliss is in the grave with thee.

But, when the days of golden dreams had perished,
And even Despair was powerless to destroy,
Then did I learn how existence could be cherished,
Strengthened, and fed without the aid of joy.

Then did I check the tears of useless passion –
Weaned my young soul from yearning after thine;

> *Sternly denied its burning wish to hasten*
> *Down to that tomb already more than mine.*
>
> *And, even yet, I dare not let it languish,*
> *Dare not indulge in memory's rapturous pain;*
> *Once drinking deep of that divinest anguish,*
> *How could I seek the empty world again?*[36]

Here, Rosina mourns how death has severed her relationship with Julius, and her anguish is heightened by the realisation that her memory will ultimately fail, thus threatening her ability to remember Julius at all. The phrase 'fifteen wild Decembers' clearly prefigures the eighteen years that Heathcliff mourned for Catherine, and the 'resting' bird sat atop the grave anticipates Edgar's visits to Catherine's grave on the anniversary of her death each year. F.R. Leavis rightly hailed this piece as the finest poem in his assessment of 19th-century verse, but it is not alone in Emily's treatment of long-lasting grief.

Similarly, in 'If grief for grief can touch thee' (1840), Emily again depicts a bereft lover addressing an absent love. It's not absolutely clear though whether this is because they have been spurned or because they are dead, yet the words poignantly convey the speaker's desperation and loneliness. The voice powerfully prefigures Heathcliff, who resembles the speaker of the poem, when, in the opening of *Wuthering Heights*, he throws open the window and calls out for Catherine, crying for her to come to him or take pity and haunt him.[37] It reads:

> *If grief for grief can touch thee,*
> *If answering woe for woe,*
> *If any ruth can melt thee*
> *Come to me now!*

I cannot be more lonely,
More drear I cannot be!
My worn heart beats so wildly
'Twill break for thee –

And when the world despises –
When heaven repels my prayer –
Will not mine angel comfort?
Mine idol hear?

Yes, by the tears I've poured,
By all my hours of pain
O I shall surely win thee,
Beloved, again![38]

The speaker's hope borders on anguish here and it's the pain of his plea that reinforces the depths of his feelings for his lost lover. But while visions of tormented love feature prominently in Emily's poetry, more hopeful expressions of romance also find expression too. 'Now trust a heart that trusts in you', from 1837, is one such piece, depicting a loyal and faithful lover who is about to depart on a voyage and offers a heartfelt farewell to his lover:

Now trust a heart that trusts in you
And firmly say the word Adieu
Be sure, wherever I may roam
My heart is with your heart at home

Unless there be no truth on earth
And vows meant true are nothing worth
And mortal man have no control
Over his own unhappy soul

Unless I change in every thought
And memory will restore me nought
And all I have of virtue die
Beneath far Gondal's Foreign sky

The mountain peasant loves the heath
Better than richest plains beneath
He would not give one moorland wild
For all the fields that ever smiled

And whiter brows than yours may be
And rosier cheeks my eyes may see
And lightning looks from orbs divine
About my pathway burn and shine

But that pure light, changeless and strong
Cherished and watched and nursed so long
That love that first its glory gave
Shall be my pole star to the grave[39]

Emily's poem is written in earnest, but from a 21st-century perspective, I can't help but find a tongue-in-cheek commentary. For instance, the male speaker romantically describes himself as a 'mountain peasant' *and* uses every romantic cliché he can find to express his feelings for his lover (declares that if there is any truth on earth, his vows of declaration are absolutely true too). But he also tells the recipient that even though there are far more beautiful people out in the world, she is a 'heath', which he 'finds dearer than tame and pleasant fields'.[40] Of course, Emily's passion for the natural world is at play here, but the words also recall so many other awkward expressions of love in literature (think Mr Darcy *and* Mr Collins in *Pride and*

Prejudice, especially in Andrew Davies' 1995 BBC adaptation, where Collins, in particular, is played so brilliantly by David Bamber to cringeworthy effect).

EMILY'S POEMS: CHARLOTTE'S EDITORIAL

In 1850, two years after Emily's death, Charlotte selected seventeen of Emily's poems to accompany a new edition of *Agnes Grey* and *Wuthering Heights*. During the process, she made numerous changes to Emily's poems, providing new titles, amending vocabulary, changing (Emily's bad) punctuation, and adding whole new sections of material. The effect of this has added to the distorted sense of Emily today. Indeed, if you do a quick internet search of some of her poems, such as 'A little while, a little while', you'll get Charlotte's much amended version pop up first, rather than Emily's original version. Consequently, this is another hazard of reading Emily's poems biographically, as a discussion of 'The Visionary' indicates.

Emily's version is a much longer prose excerpt (152 lines) from a Gondal narrative entitled 'Julian M. and A.G. Rochelle' (1845). Set during Gondal's civil war between the Royalists and the Republicans, the poem falls in two parts. In the opening (the first twelve lines), a nameless figure waits at night for a secret visitor. This then shifts to a story of the titular figures, lovers who were caught on opposites sides during Gondal's wars. Rochelle is imprisoned in a dungeon, but is visited by Julian, who is left with a troubling dilemma: either to break his former love free – 'break the chain' (line 119) – 'or seal the prisoner's woe' (120). Love-stricken, he opts for the former, and releases Rochelle, but then hides and nurses her for thirteen weeks. As a result, he concludes that:

> *By never-doubting love, unswerving constancy,*
> *Rochelle, I earned at last an equal love from thee!*[41]

Emily published the last section of the piece as 'The Prisoner' in *Poems*. Charlotte, however, reconstructed the verse. She appropriated the first twelve lines of this, added eight new lines of her own, and gave it a new title: 'The Visionary'. Consequently, a Gondal love poem was transformed into a piece that reads as a personal testimony by Emily about her literary inspiration. The piece, therefore, reads completely different:

> *Silent is the house: all are laid asleep:*
> *One alone looks out o'er the snow-wreaths deep,*
> *Watching every cloud, dreading every breeze*
> *That whirls the wildering drift, and bends the groaning trees.*
>
> *Cheerful is the hearth, soft the matted floor;*
> *Not one shivering gust creeps through pane or door;*
> *The little lamp burns straight, its rays shoot strong and far:*
> *I trim it well, to be the wanderer's guiding-star.*
>
> *Frown, my haughty sire! chide, my angry dame!*
> *Set your slaves to spy; threaten me with shame:*
> *But neither sire nor dame, nor prying serf shall know,*
> *What angel nightly tracks that waste of frozen snow.*
>
> *What I love shall come like visitant of air,*
> *Safe in secret power from lurking human snare;*
> *What loves me, no word of mine shall e'er betray,*
> *Though for faith unstained my life must forfeit pay.*

Burn, then, little lamp; glimmer straight and clear –
Hush! a rustling wing stirs, methinks, the air:
He for whom I wait, thus ever comes to me;
Strange Power! I trust thy might; trust thou my constancy.[42]

While Charlotte's editorial additions reconceived it as an autobiographical commentary on literary genius, really it reveals how *she* saw her sister: Emily's literary gifts were a divine intervention, bestowed on her, it seems, by a visitation of sorts. Problematically, this revised version is still regularly attributed to Emily. Moreover, it's given rise to 'shaky' biographical interpretations of Emily as a mystic.[43] Again, Charlotte had good intentions when handling Emily's poems. But, ultimately, these words are Charlotte's rather than Emily's.

Nonetheless, by revisiting many of Emily's poems, we do get a sense of her voice and interests and, of course, see something of the development of Ellis Bell – who would find critical acclaim through 'his' only novel, *Wuthering Heights*.

WUTHERING HEIGHTS

Today, *Wuthering Heights* is firmly recognised as a literary classic, but you wouldn't have thought this by looking at some of the early reviews. One anonymous reviewer suggested that 'it was so rude, so unfinished, and so careless, that we are perplexed to pronounce an opinion on it, or to hazard a conjecture on the future career of the author', while another more horrified critic sternly declared, 'Read *Jane Eyre* is our advice, but burn *Wuthering Heights*'.[44]

Although Charlotte's book has its share of critics, Emily's book, it seems, was a step too far for many reviewers at the time. The violence and extreme savagery she portrayed made

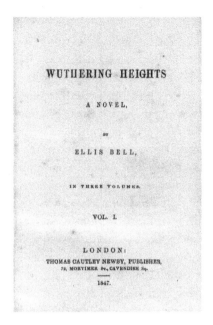

Title page of the first (1847) edition of Wuthering Heights.

it difficult for reviewers to discern an obvious moral message for readers, except for the damage brought about by obsessive passion: 'In *Wuthering Heights* the reader is shocked, disgusted, almost sickened by details of cruelty, inhumanity, and the most diabolical hate and vengeance, and anon come passages of powerful testimony to the supreme power of love – even over demons in human form'.[45]

Sadly, we don't know what Emily made of the early reviews of her novel, but she obviously read some because a handful – mostly from January 1848 – were found in her writing bureau shortly after her death. This gap in our knowledge is, of course, intriguing for fans and scholars alike who wonder why she kept just five reviews and what her reaction was to them. Hopefully,

she would have been buoyed by the fact that, despite the criti-
cisms made of her novel, many of the early reviewers applauded
her writing: 'notwithstanding its defects, we remember thinking better in its peculiar kind than anything that had been produced since the days of Fielding', wrote one anonymous reviewer
(whose review was one of the five Emily retained)[46]

The genesis of *Wuthering Heights* itself is unclear, but we do
know that because *Poems* was not a success the sisters set about
writing novels. As always in Brontë biography, there's numerous speculations offered suggesting possibilities as to the inspiration for the text. A dominant view is that Emily was likely
influenced by the wild and wonderful stories told by Tabby
Aykroyd, the much-loved domestic assistant at the parsonage.
As children, Emily and her siblings had gathered around Tabby
to hear her sensational tales of family secrets, ghostly haunt-
ings and domestic intrigue, which were most likely based on
stories that she knew from the village. It's possible that Tabby's
Gothic tales sparked Emily's imagination and she returned to
them as an adult. We can say that Tabby probably provided a
model for Ellen 'Nelly' Dean, who narrates Heathcliff's story to
Mr Lockwood and plays a prominent role in the savage family
drama. As we saw in one of the 'Diary Papers', Emily mimicked
Tabby's accent in writing, and the scribing of Yorkshire dialect
is, of course, evident in the figure of Joseph, a long-standing
servant at the Heights.

Other speculation is that Emily's novel is based on the
shifting family fortunes of the Heaton family of nearby
Ponden Hall. The Hall itself is often cited as the inspiration for
Thrushcross Grange, and Emily and her siblings probably used
the library there. A plaque that hangs above the door to the
Hall indicates that the house was reconstructed in 1801, the
year in which Emily's novel takes place. Naturally, it's possible

that Emily learned of the family's domestic dramas through Tabby, but again, we'll never know.

In his review of *Wuthering Heights*, the author and critic George Washington Peck reflected:

> *Respecting a book so original as this, and written with so much power of imagination, it is natural that there should be many opinions. Indeed, its power is so predominant that it is not easy after a hasty reading to analyse one's impressions so as to speak of its merits and demerits with confidence [.] Next to the merit of the novel as a work of thought and subtle insight, is its great power as a work of the imagination. In this respect it must rank very high, if not among the highest.*[47]

What Peck captures here is the enduring power of Emily's novel. It is, as many reviewers suggested, strange, but its those enigmatic qualities that make it so fascinating. Peck was one of the few critics to applaud Emily's skill (although his review is also quite critical of the novel's brutality, too), but the positivity with which he greets its originality stands out amidst the many opposing reviewers who thought the novel would have a short life and be quickly forgotten. Thankfully, they were wrong, and the rest, as they say, is history.

FOUR
EMILY IN NATURE

*The windswept High Sunderland Hall, near Halifax,
where Emily taught: some believe this may have been
a model for Wuthering Heights.*

Emily had an affinity with the natural world. As one biographer suggested, nowhere was she 'so much herself, nowhere else so free; nowhere else had she so many friends, wild animals living their own lives with whom she was in intense sympathetic communication'.[1] So it's apt that today the land surrounding her home on the moors (and the south Pennine hills, more broadly) is known as 'Brontë Country'. Emily was familiar with every inch of this area; she knew and loved the contours of the landscape, the hills, trees, streams, ravines, flora and fauna. Helpfully, we have eyewitness accounts of Emily's natural gaiety on the moors, as Ellen Nussey recalled how, whether she was 'on the top of the moor or in a deep glen, Emily was a child in spirit for glee and enjoyment'.[2] Ellen also reminisced of how Emily 'threw aside her reserve, and talked with freedom and vigour' during walks over the moors.[3] The Yorkshire landscape, then, was a place where Emily felt happy and independent, she gained confidence from being outside, and felt free.

It was also a realm that made her daring. There's a story that, in childhood, during one of the children's Angrian theatricals, an eleven-year-old Emily sneaked out of a second-story window at the parsonage and climbed into the branches of tree outside. But the branch gave way under her, and Emily fell to the ground. She was unhurt, but she knew her father would be displeased by the garden mischief, so the children tried to cover the damaged tree. They did a bad job, though, because Patrick noticed the damage immediately on his return home. In another tale, Ellen told how, during her walks on the moors with the sisters (which would often happen when she visited the family), Emily would sometimes lead Charlotte 'where she would not dare to go of her own free-will'.[4] Charlotte, Ellen reported, 'had a mortal dread of unknown animals, and it was Emily's pleasure to lead her into close vicinity, and then to tell her of how and of what she had done, laughing at her horror with great amusement'.[5] Poor Charlotte! Thanks to Emily's child's play she must have found herself in several uncomfortable predicaments.

With such an indelible connection with nature, it is hardly a surprise that writers and scholars over the years have also recognised how Emily's passion for the natural world formed a motif in her writing. In the early 20th century, Virginia Woolf speculated that Emily (and Charlotte) invoked 'the help of nature' because they felt 'the need of some more powerful symbol of the vast and slumbering passions in human nature than words or actions can convey'.[6] Woolf's comment helps us understand the influence of the Romantic poets on Emily, a group of writers for whom the natural world was both a setting *and* a mechanism to comment on humanity. Among this group are authors that we know the Brontës read and loved, including Byron, Robert Southey (to whom Charlotte wrote and received *that* condescending reply), and Wordsworth and Coleridge (to whom Branwell wrote with mixed results). Nature works in different ways across the work of these writers. In Wordsworth's poems, nature is revered and idealised; in Byron's verse, nature complements human emotion and helps him to make sense of civilisation; and in Keats' work, the natural world is a haven away from the grim squalor of urban living.

Like the Romantics, Emily also found that the natural world was a helpful key to understand both human nature and herself. Across her work, vivid descriptions of the environment, the seasons and the elements often provide a backdrop against which all human drama unfolds, and most of her poems begin with nature – the hills, mountains, lakes, skies or stars, for example, before moving onto human interaction and/or observation.

Sophie Franklin, in *Charlotte Brontë Revisited* (the companion title to this book), says that although many have admired 'Charlotte's particular ability to portray nature in imaginative ways', few 'have considered that this aspect of her work is bang on trend today, given the explosion of nature writing's popularity over the last few years'.[7] It's an observation that's equally applicable to Emily – if not more so.

Charlotte reflected that 'My sister Emily had a particular love for [the moors], and there is not a knoll of heather, not a branch of fern, not a young bilberry leaf not a fluttering lark or linnet but reminds me of her'.[8] I imagine that if Emily were alive to today she'd be a passionate environmental humanitarian, concerned about everything from the threat to 'green belt' land in the UK to the wider issue of global warming. While I think she'd loathe something like social media, I'd guess she would find interest in something like Instagram, where thousands of images of nature, wildlife and assorted landscapes from across the globe can be accessed instantaneously. I also believe that Emily would be a fierce advocate for animal rights.

Kirkstall Abbey, around 17 miles from Haworth, in an 1827 etching by local artist George Cuitt, who emphasised nature reclaiming the scene.

AT HOME ON THE MOORS

A visit to Haworth today will give you a very different Haworth to the one Emily lived in during the early 19th century. Today, the parsonage is an extended museum dedicated to remembering the lives and works of the Brontës, and it's sat amidst a bustling tourist industry devoted to its literary antecedents. Originally, though, the parsonage was a nine-roomed Georgian house with a stark graveyard at its front that, in Emily's day, stood at the top of the town in isolation, straddled between the town's centre and the rugged moorland, and exposed to the elements from every angle. As any Northern inhabitant knows, the Yorkshire climate changes the landscape from season to season, transforming the locale from a cold, blustery landscape in winter to a beautiful purple and green idyll in summer. No matter what the weather, though, Emily insisted on going outdoors.[9]

Indeed, the moors seemed to have beguiled Emily perpetually. In *Wuthering Heights*, the moors are often inhospitable, presenting a place of entrapment, especially for Mr Lockwood, who is, at the beginning of the novel, stranded at the Heights precisely because of the ferocious wintry conditions outside. But elsewhere in the text, the moors are a place of immense beauty *and* escape. Nelly reports that Cathy and Heathcliff would often sneak from the Heights as children to roam the moors: 'it was one of their chief amusements to runaway to the moors in the morning and remain there all day'.[10]

Along with Cathy and Heathcliff, the image of Emily energetically traversing the moors remains equally popular. Locals often remembered Emily 'whistling to her dogs, and taking long-strides over the rough earth', and parishioners in the church beside her home recalled viewing her through its windows, heading off over the rugged terrain.[11] Rather annoyingly, this same image has also informed the stubborn myth that Emily was a mystic. To me, this just says that she loved walking; it was 'a necessity for Emily' and a 'near-daily ritual'.[12] Importantly, visitors to Haworth today can literally walk in Emily's footsteps, hiking across the Pennines to Peniston Craggs, a place that draws Cathy's attention in *Wuthering Heights*, or visit Top Withins, the location that perhaps inspired the ominous titular property, which is approximately three and a half miles from the parsonage. Also on this route lies a secluded spot favoured by Emily and Anne that they dubbed 'the Meeting of the Waters'. Ellen Nussey described this as:

> *a small oasis of emerald green turf, broken here and there by small clear springs; a few large stones served as resting places; seated here we were hidden from the world, nothing appearing in view but miles and miles of heather, a glorious blue sky, and brightening sun. A fresh breeze wafted on us its exhilarating influence; we laughed and made mirth of each other, and settled we would call ourselves the Quartette. Emily, half reclining on a slab of stone, played like a young child with the tadpoles in the water, making them swim about, and then fell to moralising on the strong and the weak, the brave and the cowardly, as she chased them with her hand.*[13]

Patrick and Branwell were voracious walkers too, and the family's pedestrianism finds expression in *Wuthering Heights*. Mr Earnshaw's extended sixty-mile walk to Liverpool is redolent of Patrick's long walks. In the novel, Earnshaw's walk is of great significance, for it is from this journey that he arrives home with Heathcliff. The critic John Sutherland has humorously pondered why Earnshaw would choose to do this near treble marathon on foot when clearly there were horses available in the stable.[14] Hmm. One obvious answer is that he really liked walking too.

It's this passion for walking and nature that gave Emily the solitude she craved, so it's apt that Charlotte described her sister as a 'solitude-loving raven'.[15] As we've seen, Emily's penchant for solitude and her infamous reserve were received awkwardly by others, making her unconventional in her day. But as Charlotte indicated, on her own on the moors Emily felt free:

> *My sister Emily loved the moors. Flowers brighter than the rose bloomed in the blackest of the heath for her; out of a sullen hollow in a lived hill-side her mind could make an Eden. She found in the bleak solitude many and dear delighted; and not the least and best loved was – liberty.*[16]

The image of a lone woman (and her dogs) striding defiantly across the Yorkshire moorland is incredibly powerful to me; Emily was an independent spirit at a time when female independence wasn't culturally welcomed, and it's partly for that reason that she's cruelly derided as odd and weird. But Emily clearly was not vexed by the judgment of others, and walking literally and metaphorically energised her sense of self. The following poem captures this sentiment. Although some have speculated on its authorship, it's commonly attributed to Emily:

> *Often rebuked, yet always back returning*
> *To those first feelings that were born with me,*
> *And leaving busy chase of wealth and learning*
> *For idle dreams of things which cannot be:*

Today, I will seek not the shadowy region;
  Its unsustaining vastness waxes drear;
And visions rising, legion after legion,
  Bring the unreal world too strangely near.

I'll walk, but not in old heroic traces,
  And not in paths of high morality,
And not among the half-distinguish'd faces,
  The clouded forms of long-past history.

I'll walk when my own nature would be leading:
  It vexes me to choose another guide:
Where the grey flocks in ferny glens are feeding,
  Where the wild wind blows on the mountain side.

What have those lonely mountains worth revealing?
  More glory and more grief that I can tell:
The earth that wakes one human heart to feeling
  Can centre both the worlds of Heaven and Hell.[17]

SEASONS AND STARS

Emily's solitary walks also allowed her to do something else, namely, observe nature. As an adult, Emily's room in the parsonage was a small one at the top of the stairs, but it had a huge window beneath which her bed was placed. She probably lay at night looking up at the sky and watching the stars, and this imagery is found in her poem 'Stars' (1846):[18]

Ah! why, because the dazzling sun
  Restored our earth to joy

Emily in Nature

Have you departed, every one,
    And left a desert sky?

All through the night, your glorious eyes
    Were gazing down in mine,
And with a full heart's thankful sighs
    I blessed that watch divine!

I was at peace, and drank your beams
    As they were life to me
And revelled in my changeful dreams
    Like petrel on the sea.

Thought followed thought, star followed star
    Through boundless regions, on;
While one sweet influence, near and far,
    Thrilled through, and proved us one.

Why did the morning dawn to break
    So great, so pure a spell;
And scorch with fire, the tranquil cheek
    Where your cool radiance fell?

Blood-red, he rose, and arrow-straight
    His fierce beams struck my brow;
The soul of Nature, sprang, elate,
    But mine sank sad and low!

My lids closed down, yet through their veil,
    I saw him blazing, still,
And steep in gold the misty dale,
    And flash upon the hill.

I turned me to the pillow, then,
  To call back night, and see
Your worlds of solemn light, again,
  Throb with my heart, and me!

It would not do – the pillow glowed
  And glowed both roof and floor;
And birds sang loudly in the wood,
  And fresh winds shook the door.

The curtains waved, the wakened flies
  Were murmuring round my room,
Imprisoned there, till I should rise
  And give them leave to roam.

Oh, stars, and dreams and, gentle night;
  Oh, night and stars return!
And hide me from the hostile light,
  That does not warm, but burn;

That drains the blood of suffering men;
  Drinks tears, instead of dew;
Let me sleep through his blinding reign,
  And only wake with you![19]

In this poem, the speaker professes her love for the stars at night while critiquing the rise of the 'red blood' sun that disrupts the peace and tranquillity of night-time. The influence of the stars is apparent here (the beams from the star were 'life to me') and suggests that stars opened up Emily's imagination (in the same way that the sky is filled with star after star). Moreover, this love is reciprocal: the speaker is gazing lovingly at the stars, but their 'glorious eyes' beam back at her. A peaceful image.

The contemporary poet Anne Carson has also picked up on Emily's passion for observation in her homage to the Brontës entitled 'The Glass Essay'. In her extended poem, Carson pictures Emily as a watcher, but she deliberately misspells it as 'whacher' because that's how Emily (mis)spelt it in the few sources of her writing that remain:

> *She whached God and humans and moor wind and open night.*
> *She whached eyes, stars, inside, outside, actual weather.*
>
> *She whached the bars of time, which broke.*
> *She whached the poor core of the world, wide open.*[20]

Reading Emily's poems, it's clear that her natural ability for close observation finds expression in her repeated depiction of the seasons, with winter being one that she frequently returns to. Without electricity or heat, the arrival of winter in Haworth would certainly have been a 'grim event' in the 19th century, hence its usual association with death, sadness and hardship in Emily's work.[21] Her poem 'The blue bell is the sweetest flower' offers such a view; the speaker laments the absence of flowers in winter, particularly the bluebell, because it holds such power over her spirit:

> *The blue bell is the sweetest flower*
> *That waves in summer air:*
> *Its blossoms have the mightiest power*
> *To soothe my spirit's care.*
>
> *There is a spell in purple heath*
> *Too wildly, sadly dear*

The violet has a fragrant breath,
But fragrance will not cheer,

The trees are bare, the sun is cold,
And seldom, seldom seen –
The heavens have lost their zone of gold
And earth her robe of green

And ice upon the glancing stream
Has cast its sombre shade
And distant hills and valleys seem
In frozen mist arrayed –

The blue bell cannot charm me now
The heath has lost its bloom
The violets in the glen below
They yield no sweet perfume

But, though I mourn the heather-bell,
'Tis better far away
I know how fast my tears would swell
To see it smile today

And that wood flower that hides so shy
Beneath the mossy stone
Its balmy scent and dewy eye
'Tis not for them I moan

It is the slight and stately stem
The blossom's silvery blue
The buds hid like a sapphire gem
In sheaths of emerald hue

'Tis these that breathe upon my heart
A calm and softening spell
That if it makes the tear-drop start
Has power to soothe as well

For these I weep, so long divided
Through winter's dreary day
In longing weep – but most when guided
On withered banks to stray

If chilly then the light should fall
Adown the dreary sky
And gild the dank and darkened wall
With transient brilliancy

How do I yearn, how do I pine
For the time of flowers to come
And turn me from that fading shine
To mourn the fields of home –[22]

Emily wrote this poem on 18 December 1838, and the speaker's sorrow towards the mutability of the seasons is notable, with the absence of bluebells providing a focal point for what we nowadays call the 'winter blues'. Interestingly, though, eleven days earlier, Emily had written another poem that offers an alternate view of winter in which she celebrates the colder time of year as one of great beauty:

How still, how happy! those are words
That once would scarce agree together
I loved the plashing of the surge –
The changing heaven the breezy weather,

More than smooth seas and cloudless skies
And solemn, soothing, softened airs
That in the forest woke no sighs
And from the green spray shook no tears.

How still, how happy! now I feel
Where silence dwells is sweeter far
Than laughing mirth's most joyous swell
However pure its raptures are.

Come, sit down on this sunny stone:
'Tis wintry light o'er flowerless moors –
But sit – for we are all alone
And clear expand heaven's breathless shores.

I could think in the withered grass
Spring's budding wreaths we might discern
The violet's eye might shyly flash
And young leaves shoot among the fern.

It is but thought – full many a night
The snow shall clothe those hills afar
And storms shall add a drearier blight
And winds shall wage a wilder war,

Before the lark may herald in
Fresh foliage twined with blossoms fair
And summer days again begin
Their glory – haloed crown to wear.

> *Yet my heart loves December's smile*
> *As much as July's golden beam;*
> *Then let us sit and watch the while*
> *The blue ice curdling on the stream* –[23]

Here, the speaker invites someone (it's not clear who) to sit with them and admire the silent tranquillity of a winter's day. Even though the light is 'wintry' and the moors are 'flowerless', the speaker still finds beauty in the bleak locale. The speaker recognises that hints of spring are beginning to be discernible to the eye (and spring, of course, is the time of nature's rebirth), but says that there's pleasure to be found in 'December's smile' too, that's equal, in its own way, to 'July's golden beam'.[24] Although Emily's thoughts on winter changes across these two poems, what's really interesting is how they are connected with emotion.

Alongside the seasons, the elements feature prominently in Emily's work, with the wind, of course, holding a particularly dominant place in her writing, as the title of her novel, *Wuthering Heights*, indicates. 'Wuthering', as the character Lockwood tells us, is

> *a significant provincial adjective, descriptive of the atmospheric tumult to which its station is exposed in stormy weather. Pure, bracing ventilation they must have up there, at all times, indeed: one may guess the power of the north wind, blowing over the edge, by the excessive slant of a few, stunted firs at the end of the house; and by a range of gaunt thorns all stretching their limbs one way, as if craving alms of the sun. Happily, the architect had foresight to build it strong: the narrow windows are deeply set in the wall, and the corners defended with large jutting stones.*[25]

Several critics have noted that Wuthering Heights was perhaps based on a yeoman house called High Sunderland located
near Law Hill, the school in Halifax where Emily taught in
1838.[26] Hilda Marsden's writing on the novel's scenic background explores in detail the parallel between Emily's descriptions and High Sunderland, and makes a persuasive case for
its influence.[27] But the lines equally remind me of the parsonage. In Emily's day, the family must also have felt and heard the
bracing northern wind rushing around it on its lonely position
at the top of the town, and I imagine that at times the rushing
would have been rather scary, especially in storms, or worse,
hurricanes!

Like the stars, in her poems the wind is often a prop to open
the imagination, as 'The Night Wind' (1840) indicates:

In summer's mellow midnight
A cloudless moon shone through
Our open parlour window
And rose-trees wet with dew

I sat in silent musing –
The soft wind waved my hair
It told me Heaven was glorious
And sleeping Earth was fair

I needed not its breathing
To bring such thoughts to me
But still it whispered lowly
'How dark the woods will be! –

'The thick leaves in my murmur
Are rustling like a dream,

And all their myriad voices
Instinct with spirit seem.'

I said, 'Go, gentle singer,
Thy wooing voice is kind:
But do not think its music
Has power to reach my mind –

'Play with the scented flower,
The young tree's supple bough –
And leave my human feelings
In their own course to flow.'

The wanderer would not heed me;
Its kiss grew warmer still –
'O come!' it sighed so sweetly
'I'll win thee 'gainst thy will -

'Were we not friends from childhood?
Have I not loved thee long?
As long as thou hast loved the night,
Whose silence wakes my song?

'And when thy heart is laid to rest
Beneath the church-yard stone
I shall have time for mourning,
And thou to be alone.' [28]

In the poem, the speaker converses with the wind, whose 'wooing' sound hypnotically calls her to day-dream, thus luring her into her imagination. The action takes place at midnight during the summer, when the 'cloudless moon' shines powerfully through the speaker's window as well as through the rose bushes in the garden. Interestingly, in the Honresfeld manuscript, Emily dated the poem 11 September 1848 and, as Janet Gezari has reported, on that night in Haworth, the moon was a full one *and* the wind was blowing.[29] We can surmise, then, that the summer wind and brightness of the moon maybe kept Emily awake or inspired her to get up at midnight and compose this verse, which suggests that her creative imagination was something she meditated over even when she went to bed at night.

ANIMAL BONDS

Alongside the landscape and all of its earthly components, a significant part of Emily's intimacy with the natural world was her 'passion' for animals (a term Gaskell used).[30] She was an animal lover and held them in high regard; higher, it's said, than she often regarded humans, as Gaskell reported sneeringly.[31] Her Diary Papers teem with reports of the animals she kept at the parsonage (it must have been something of a menagerie, and Emily Dr Dolittle), and they definitely inspired Emily's creative imagination beyond writing, something we see in her art.

Take, for instance, her beautiful 1841 watercolour of her pet merlin, Nero, so named presumably because his wild ways (a bird of prey) evoked those of the tyrannical emperor. Emily rescued the injured Nero from the moors and brought him back to the parsonage to tend his injuries. She developed a close bond with him and his striking beauty led her to capture his image on paper. The piece is stunning and shows off her skill for close observation. Indeed, his plumage is *so* delicately rendered that it's easy to imagine him raising his wings and flying off the page. Looking at Nero's image it's hard to understand

Emily's 1841 watercolour of Nero, the magnificent merlin she rescued and reared, shows her close observation to the creature's form and plumage.

why Clement Shorter commented that 'Emily's taste for drawing is a pathetic element in her always pathetic life' and that most of Emily's drawings are 'technically full of errors'.[32] I disagree wholeheartedly (and how rude!) and Nero's portrait suggests otherwise.

Of all the animals that lived with the family, though, it's Keeper, Emily's dog, who has a special place in her biography. Keeper was a gift to Emily, but we don't know who from. He was a huge bullmastiff and you can get a sense of just *how* big he was from his collar, which is housed in the Parsonage Museum. Really, his name tells us everything we need to know about Emily's affection for her dog; he was a keeper. As well as accompanying her for daily walks on the moors, Keeper could be found lying next to Emily on the carpet while she read. Apparently, she often had to adjust her own position to reciprocate his affection, manoeuvring herself to get her arm around his big neck. Hilariously, despite his size, he seemed to have thought of himself as something of a lapdog because he worked hard to cuddle up on his mistress' lap, often pushing Charlotte aside just so he could be with Emily.[33] Charlotte transported the relationship between Emily and Keeper into her second novel, *Shirley*, where Emily appears as Shirley and Keeper as 'Tartar':

> *The tawny and lionlike bulk of Tartar is ever stretched beside her, his negro muzzle laid on his fore paws – straight, strong, and shapely as the limbs of an Alpine wolf. One hand of his mistress generally reposes on the loving serf's rude head, because if she takes it away he groans and is discontented.*[34]

Like Nero, Keeper was also a muse for Emily's art. Alongside a rough sketch of him by her side in one of her Diary Papers, a striking portrait from 1838 can be found at the Parsonage Museum, and he appears in drawings alongside Flossy (Anne's dog) and the house cat, Tiger.

It's thanks to Gaskell, though, that a more troubling narrative about Emily and her Keeper continues to circulate. In *The Life of Charlotte Brontë*, Gaskell asserted that Keeper 'loved' to sneak to parts of the house where he wasn't allowed; stealing upstairs, for instance, when no one was looking and jumping up on the beds, stretching his 'square, tawny limbs on the comfortable bed' and ruining the clean white counterpanes.[35] Tabby, the parsonage housekeeper, wasn't impressed by the dog's habit, and in reply to one of 'Tabby's remonstrances' Gaskell reports how Emily 'declared that, if he was found again transgressing, she herself, in defiance of warning and his well-known ferocity of nature, would beat him so severely that he would never offend again'.[36] Accordingly, that's just what happened, or so says Gaskell:

> *In the gathering dusk of an autumn evening, Tabby came, half-triumphantly, half-trembling, but in great wrath, to tell Emily Keeper was lying on the bed, in drowsy voluptuousness. Charlotte saw Emily's whitening face, and set mouth, but dared not speak to interfere; no one dared when Emily's eyes glowed in that manner out of the paleness of her face, and when her lips were so compressed into stone. She went upstairs, and Tabby and Charlotte stood in the gloomy passage below, full of the dark shadows of the coming night. Down-stairs came Emily, dragging after her the unwilling Keeper, his hind legs set in the heavy attitude of resistance, held by the 'scruff of his neck,' but growling low and savagely all the time. The watchers would fain have spoken, but durst not, for fear of taking off Emily's attention, and causing her to avert her head for a moment from the enraged brute. She let him go, planted in a dark corner at the bottom of the stairs; no time was there to fetch stick or rod, for fear of the strangling clutch at her throat – her bare clenched fist struck against his red fierce eyes, before he had time to make his spring, and, in the language of the turf, she 'punished him' til his eyes were swelled up, and the half-blind, stupefied beast was led to his accustomed lair, to have his swollen head fomented and cared for by the very Emily herself. The generous dog owed her no grudge; he loved her dearly ever after.[37]*

The suggestion that Emily beat her dog's face to a pulp is sensational and shocking, and the lurid detail that Gaskell employs ensures that it resurfaces from time-to-time in scholarship and beyond. In the tabloid media, it's clickbait. 'Emily Brontë beat up her dog', states a *Daily Mail* headline from a 2015 article; 'The Animalistic Emily Brontë and Her Dog, Keeper' runs another.[38] But I think it is another of Gaskell's over-zealous embellishments; or, actually, outright falsehood, and I hold this view for several reasons. I want to labour over it briefly because it has become a stubborn part of 'Emily folklore'.

In the first place, as we have already seen, Gaskell disliked Emily even though she never met her. In *The Brontë Myth*, Lucasta Miller astutely evaluates Gaskell's shocking anecdote and also finds it wanting. Miller notes how Gaskell's colourful prose presents 'it as vividly as though she were actually there':

Emily's portrait of her beloved dog, Keeper.

> *[Emily's] glowing eyes are identified with Keeper's 'red fierce*
> *eyes', as though the two were members of the same animal*
> *species. He does not merely 'growl', he growls 'savagely'. In*
> *fact, he is no longer a dog but a 'brute', whose home is not*
> *a kennel but a 'lair'. Nor is Emily any longer a woman: she*
> *is a pugilist, whom only the 'language of the turf' will suit.*
> *Having punished the animal, Emily reverts to a conven-*
> *tionally feminine nurturing role to bathe his wounds, but*
> *this only heightens the Jekyll-and-Hyde effect.*[39]

Indeed, not only was Gaskell 'not there', but the origins of the incident are obscure and, as Miller points out, there's reason to question if it took place at all. For Gaskell, the story complements the violent image she has of Emily's *Wuthering Heights*, so she constructs a dual between Keeper and Emily in which Emily must become a sadistic 'beast in a woman's body'.[40]

Gaskell's representation of Emily's violent overreaction also sits counter to everything else we *do* know (for certain) about Emily and her relationship to animals. Emily, we've seen, filled the house with all kinds of creatures: cats, dogs, geese – which she tamed and named after the then Queen and the Queen Mother, 'Victoria' and 'Adelaide' – and other birds and wildlife that she found during her walks, saw were injured and brought home to rehabilitate back to health. In this respect, she's more akin to a veterinary nurse or zoological rehabilitator than a violent animal abuser. Even Anne and Charlotte's report that Emily grieved over the death of a family cat, 'an animal so pampered that it seemed to have lost a cat's nature and subsided into luxurious amiability and contentment', reinforces Emily's deep sensitivity to animals and suffering.[41]

Moreover, there are several accounts of her breaking up a dogfight in the town (much to the consternation of the locals who stood around watching) *and* another where she helped a poorly dog that had run 'past the parsonage with its head lolling and its tongue hanging out'.[42] On this occasion, Emily was trying to give the suffering hound some water, but it was obviously scared and anxious (probably caused from human violence if people thought it was a rabid stray), and it snapped at her arm, drawing blood. Emily, it's said, 'went straight to the kitchen' and used a red-hot iron from the fire to cauterise the wound herself, and it is likely she developed erysipelas from it (a red, painful inflammation that results in severe bilious attacks and general weakness).[43] The ever-stoic Emily told no one of the incident, probably fearing that her family would over-react and make an intolerable fuss about the whole thing (or indeed, harp on about the lengths she went to in order to care for animals), but she eventually conceded and Charlotte represented it in *Shirley*. If anything, these narratives show that Emily was extremely passionate about animal welfare and quite happy to put the well-being of animals before herself.

A final reason I'm dubious about Gaskell's report is because of Emily's emotional response to nature. As Deborah Lutz comments, animals 'opened up a well of emotion' in Emily, 'something humans rarely did'.[44] Indeed, in most of her writings, Emily invokes the predatory impulse of the natural world to comment on the violence of humanity, something she was deeply critical of. She felt that animals were 'more honest in their expression of their natures' and this 'made them superior to humans'.[45] Such a view is controversial for many, especially to those who perceive it as 'anti-humanist'.[46] Emily's concern for the brutality of humanity is expressed in one of her *devoirs*, entitled '*Le Chat*' (The Cat). The pleasant title was one that

Héger thought appropriate for French composition, but in Emily's hands it was turned into a philosophical treatise.[47] In it, Emily makes clear her view on animals and humans: people are most like cats in their excessive hypocrisy, cruelty and ingratitude. The short essay, written on 15 May 1842, is reproduced here in full, and it displays Emily's rhetorical skill and knack for constructing an argument through contrasting statements:

> *I can say with sincerity that I like cats; also I can give very good reasons why those who despise them are wrong.*
>
> *A cat is an animal who has more human feelings than almost any other being. We cannot sustain a comparison with the dog, it is infinitely too good; but the cat, although it differs in some physical points, is extremely like us in disposition.*
>
> *There may be people, in truth, who would say that this resemblance extends only to the most wicked men; that it is limited to their excessive hypocrisy, cruelty, and ingratitude; detestable vices in our race and equally odious in that of cats.*
>
> *Without disputing the limits that those individuals set on our affinity, I answer that if hypocrisy, cruelty, and ingratitude are exclusively the domain of the wicked, that class comprises everyone. Our education develops one of those qualities in great perfection; the others flourish without nurture, and far from condemning them, we regard all three with great complacency. A cat, in its own interest, sometimes hides its misanthropy under the guise of amiable gentleness; instead of tearing what it desires from its master's hand, it approaches with a caressing air, rubs its pretty little head against him, and advances a paw whose touch is soft as down. When it has gained its end,*

it resumes its character of Timon; and that artfulness in it is called hypocrisy. In ourselves, we give it another name, politeness, and he who did not use it to hide his real feelings would soon be driven from society.

'But,' says some delicate lady, who has murdered a half-dozen lapdogs through pure affection, 'the cat is such a cruel beast, he is not content to kill his prey, he torments it before its death; you cannot make that accusation against us.' More or less, Madame. Your husband, for example, likes hunting very much, but foxes being rare on his land, he would not have the means to pursue this amusement often, it he did not manage his supplies thus: once he has run an animal to its last breath, he snatches it from the jaws of the hounds and saves it to suffer the same infliction two or three more times, ending finally in death. You yourself avoid the bloody spectacle because it wounds your weak nerves. But I have seen you embrace your child in transports, when he came to show you a beautiful butterfly crushed between his cruel fingers; and at that moment, I really wanted to have a cat, with the tail of a half-devoured rat hanging from its mouth, to present as the image, the true copy, of your angel. You could not refuse to kiss him, and if he scratches us both in revenge, so much the better. Little boys are rather liable to acknowledge their friends' caresses in that way, and the resemblance would be more perfect. They know how to value our favours at their true price, because they guess the motives that prompt us to grant them, and if those motives might sometimes be good, undoubtedly they remember always that they owe all their misery and all their evil qualities to the great ancestor of humankind. For assuredly, the cat was not wicked in Paradise.[48]

Anne Brontë, in a sketch by Charlotte.

Clearly, Emily had strong opinions about polite society and her conviction lacks sentiment towards humanity. Instead, she's concerned with attacking conventional (and somewhat hypocritical) social attitudes towards human *and* animal nature, asking the imagined Madame if she would kiss a cat with a half-eaten rat's tail spilling out of its mouth. Several readers have commented on the perverse pleasure in this grim image, but it's really an alternate way of addressing what her sister, Anne, wrote about in *Agnes Grey*, when the titular governess is shocked and appalled to find that the petted son of the household in which she works is preparing to torture a nestful of young birds to death.

In '*Le Chat*', Emily points out that humans are often duplicitous, cruel and self-interested. Stevie Davies believes the piece shows evidence that Emily anticipated what we now call social Darwinism, the idea that people are subject to the same rules that Darwin suggested existed in the natural world. If this is the case – and I think there's a lot of truth to this – then it's unlikely that Emily would have beaten up Keeper, for logically that would be a power-driven and perverse human intervention on animal nature. There's a lot to be said about Emily, but the story of her beating Keeper is, I think, just that: a story.

In truth, Emily valued animals, and nature in general – she revered its beauty and freedoms, even its volatility, something we saw in her poetic account of the bog burst she witnessed in childhood. For Emily, nature wasn't something to be used and abused, nor was it a metaphor to prop up fiction; it was something to be held in the highest regard. Being at one with nature, supporting and preserving it, were values that Emily treasured. For me, this makes her more – not less – human, and her attitude would sit comfortably alongside animal lovers and environmentalists today.

FIVE

EMILY AND FEMINISM

Emily Jane Brontë May the 2nd 1829

'I am no bird; and no net ensnares me: I am a free human
being with an independent will.' So said Charlotte's title
character Jane Eyre. But how much was this true of Emily?

'Why all the fuss? She wanted liberty. Well didn't she have it? A reasonably satisfactory home life, a most satisfactory dream-life – why then all this beating of wings? What was this cage, invisible to us, which she felt herself to be confined in?' So said Cecil Day Lewis in 1957.[1] The horror he expresses in this article (published in *Brontë Society Transactions*, now *Brontë Studies*) towards the idea women might dream of something more than domesticity seems rather humorous today. But, sadly, it's also indicative of the way in which, historically, especially in the mid-19th century, a woman's place was considered to be in the home. The Brontës wrote at a time during which the ideology of separate spheres was dominant in middle-class households. While women were said to govern the domestic sphere, men had far more freedom, enjoying life in the public world. Theirs was a world of education, medicine, science, travel, employment, business, the military and government. Women had no such power nor were their attempts to leave their 'proper' place welcomed, as Cecil Day Lewis' comment indicates.

Within the history of feminism, then, the Brontës have an important place. Their works come after the 'birth' of feminism, which is nominally marked as the publication of Mary Wollstonecraft's *A Vindication of the Rights of Woman* in 1792, but before the advent of the first wave of feminism in the late 19th century, which focused on women's legal emancipation. Charlotte's *Jane Eyre* is considered by many to be an early feminist novel, and readings of the text have been enriched since the rise of literary feminisms led by critics such as Sandra Gilbert and Susan Gubar in the late 1970s.

Anne's work too, especially *The Tenant of Wildfell Hall*, has long been recognised (probably much to Charlotte's horror) as a feminist manifesto of sorts. Yet, for some reason,

despite the work of feminist critics, such as Lynn Pykett and
Stevie Davies, both of whom have provided rich insights into
Emily's gender agenda, she's not so readily recognised as a
feminist in the same manner as her sisters. One reason for
this is that, as Davies notes, Emily was 'publicly silent' about
'feminist social issues on which her sisters took up outspoken
positions'.[2] What Davies indicates here is that neither Emily's
poetry nor *Wuthering Heights* include such an impassioned
speech as that spoken by Jane to Mr Rochester in Charlotte's
novel:

> *Do you think, because I am poor, obscure, plain, and little,*
> *I am soulless and heartless? You think wrong! – I have as*
> *much soul as you, – and full as much heart! And if God*
> *had gifted me with some beauty and much wealth, I should*
> *have made it as hard for you to leave me, as it is now for*
> *me to leave you. I am not talking to you now through the*
> *medium of custom, conventionalities, nor even of mortal*
> *flesh; – it is my spirit that addresses your spirit; just as if*
> *both had passed through the grave, and we stood at God's*
> *feet, equal, – as we are!*[3]

Neither does Emily's writing reveal any feminist declaration as offered by Anne in her preface to the second edition of
The Tenant of Wildfell Hall: 'if I have warned one rash youth
from following in their steps, or prevented one thoughtless
girl from falling into the very natural error of my heroine,
the book has not been written in vain.'[4] But I disagree with
Davies and think that Emily was a feminist (or more properly,
protofeminist) and her work is, despite views to the contrary,
readily accessible as such. It is just presented differently to
her sisters.

EMILY'S MASCULINITY

Gender seems to have been at the forefront of Emily's life, and biographical fragments about her often indicate this. For instance, Constantin Héger famously remarked that Emily 'should have been a man – a great navigator'.[5] Héger was praising Emily's intellect, but he uses masculine imagery to do so. His comment indicates how clever women, were (and are) rarely seen as feminine because intellectualism is oppositional to femininity, apparently. Sigh!

Interestingly, Charlotte drew further attention to Emily's masculinity in her fictionalisation of her sister in *Shirley*, where Emily appears in the guise of the land-owning heiress who knows how to handle herself with a gun. Shirley's known as

An extremely assertive Shirley in an 1897 edition of Charlotte's novel.

'Captain Keelder' by many of the traditional male characters, who perceive her power and privilege (as well as her use of them) as more masculine than feminine. The novel's other female main character, Caroline Helstone, also values Shirley's 'masculinity', relying on her for guidance and accompaniment in challenging situations. Today the name 'Shirley' is a stereotypically female one, but in the 19th century it was a boy's name. In the novel, Shirley is so named because her parents had anticipated a boy, but when she turned out to be a girl they called her Shirley anyway.

What these points tell us is that Emily was clearly an atypical woman. She rejected the traits usually associated with femininity – such as passivity, emotion, irrationality. The skewed logic that's at play, then, is that if Emily wasn't womanly, she must have been more of a man, at which point I can almost hear the collective sigh from feminists reading Emily from across the generations.

Gender isn't viewed like this anymore and today Emily wouldn't be seen as inherently masculine (or 'manly'). Thanks to many years of feminism, diversity among women is accepted and feminism has pushed back against the dominant ideas that once deemed what was 'normal' for a woman to do or achieve. As such, in 21st-century culture, there's no one singular notion of what it means to be a woman; rather, there are lots of different women and lots of different types of women and femininities – including more masculine ones. Today, strong, gutsy women – like Emily – are valued in society. Just think of the famous Second World War propaganda image of Rosie the Riveter, whose bicep curl sits rather comfortably alongside her eyeliner, lipstick and retro hair scarf tied in vintage mid-century fashion, accompanied by the famous slogan 'We can do it'.

Importantly, one of the few commentators who seems to have anticipated and appreciated Emily's 'masculinity' was John Greenwood, the Haworth stationer. For most of his life, Greenwood kept a diary of events from Haworth, and he documented an occasion when Emily's physical strength and defiance of gender was both needed *and* valued by the villagers. According to Greenwood, a local rushed up to the parsonage to tell Emily that Keeper and 'another great powerful dog out of the village were fighting' out in the street.[6] According to Greenwood, Emily

> *never spoke a word, nor appeared the least at a loss what to do, but rushed at once into the kitchen, took the pepper box, and away into the lane where she found the two savage brutes each holding the other by the throat...while several other animals, who thought themselves men, were standing looking like cowards...watching this fragile creature spring upon the beasts – seizing Keeper round the neck with one arm, while with the other hand she dredges well their noses with pepper, and separating them by force of her great will.*[7]

Greenwood's full of praise for Emily. He clearly admired her quick-witted and resourceful action, even pitting her response against anything offered by the men of the town who, by contrast, seemed cowardly in the face of fighting dogs. As Pykett has commented, it's important to note that Greenwood conceptualises Emily's 'masculinity' in 'a language of competence and practicality': she 'outshines the men of the village' *and* debunks 19th-century gender norms in such a triumphant manner.[8] She's not a man, but a strong and very capable woman.

Of course, because Emily does not easily fit with 'normal' definitions of womanhood, it's unsurprising to find that her fictional representations of women resist easy categorisation too. As we've seen, in the fantasy world of Gondal, Emily's female creations are bold, ambitious and emancipated rebels who frequently usurp traditional gender roles. By choosing to structure Gondal around Augusta (A.G.A.), Emily (and Anne) overtly played with images of gender, power and politics. For Winifred Gérin, Emily's biographer, this in itself also registers something else:

> *When Emily called her heroine 'Augusta' she was not only asserting her regal status, but commenting on the known fact that the name had been refused the Princess Victoria at her baptism by her uncle George IV because it had sounded ominously imperious in his ears. Emily moreover gave the princess's first name, Alexandrina, to another of her heroines.*[9]

The Queen's coronation clearly made an impact on Emily since she also later named a goose after her. However, while Emily may have seen some form of solidarity and sisterhood with the newly crowned princess, we should remember that Victoria was not quite an overt feminist icon, as remarks she made in 1870 indicate:

> *The Queen is most anxious to enlist everyone who can speak or write to join in checking this mad, wicked folly of 'Woman's Rights,' with all its attendant horrors, on which her poor feeble sex is bent, forgetting every sense of womanly feeling and propriety [...] It is a subject which makes the Queen so furious that she cannot contain herself. God*

*created men and women different – then let them remain
each in their own position. Tennyson has some beautiful
lines on the difference of men and women in 'The Princess'.
Woman would become the most hateful, heartless, and
disgusting of human beings were she allowed to unsex herself; and where would be the protection which man was
intended to give the weaker sex?*[10]

Victoria's comments seem rather humorous in retrospect
and are decidedly outdated today. But irrespective of Queen
Victoria's feminist perspective, Emily gives *her* leading women,
in the Gondal poems, an awareness of how women with power
can be pejoratively viewed, as these lines from 'The Death of
A.G.A.' indicate:

*One was a woman tall and fair;
A princess she might be
From her stately form and her features rare
And her look of majesty –*

*But on, she had a sullen frown –
A lip of cruel scorn –
As sweet tears never melted down
Her cheeks since she was born!*[11]

Emily's high-spirited and independent women, then, are
rarely broken, but what's really interesting is that she often uses
female subjects to explore the nature of selfhood. Several critics
who have studied Emily's poems have noted that she regularly
returns to the idea of being true to oneself. In *Wuthering
Heights*, this issue sits at the forefront of Catherine Earnshaw's
story. For Catherine, the need to be true to oneself is challenged

by gender roles, especially the rigidity of femininity, and in the course of the novel we see how she resists female norms (for a time, at least) and how the whole matter becomes an emotional quandary for her.

In her younger years, Catherine is never happier than when she's romping about on the moors barefoot with her Heathcliff. But later, as an adult, she's 'forced' to become a genteel lady. As a result, her newfound status means that it would degrade her 'now' to marry Heathcliff, but this doesn't stop her from declaring to Nelly her famous words 'I am Heathcliff' or that he is 'more myself than I am'.[12] Cathy's comment to Nelly Dean is often read primarily as expressive of love and a commentary on Catherine's affinity to her underdog sibling, Heathcliff; their love is intense but not socially sanctioned. But when read solely in relation to gender, the comment also raises a question about how we understand ourselves and how gender often informs our sense of identity.

Writing in 1979, the famous feminist literary critics Sandra Gilbert and Susan Gubar read Catherine's statement as one of androgyny: she negates her own femininity and appears sexless. But as I see it, Catherine's statement is a rejection of femininity in favour of masculinity precisely because genteel femininity is too restricting for her. Cathy's words don't imply that she wants to *be* a man, though; rather, being a woman is too constricting. She recognises this, and so, this is how she expresses her resistance.

In many ways, there's an affinity here between the active 'I' in Catherine's declaration and Jane's at the end of *Jane Eyre*, when she memorably declares, 'Reader, I married him'.[13] As many have noted, it's Jane doing the marrying (as her 'I' indicates): she's marrying Rochester, rather than he is marrying Jane. In *Wuthering Heights*, Emily does the same sort of thing: Cathy is the active agent: she *is* Heathcliff, not he is Cathy. In other words, she identifies with Heathcliff as a man, rather than he identifies with her. And this tells us that Cathy's experience of femininity is one that imposes a limit on her. In this respect, it wouldn't be hard to imagine her speaking the other often quoted words of Charlotte's protagonist: 'I desired liberty; for liberty I gasped; for liberty I uttered a prayer.'[14] But in the 19th century, non-feminine women weren't all that welcomed, so it's unsurprising that Cathy has no option to but to become a 'proper' woman.

Perhaps when writing these scenes, Emily recalled the teasing comments made to her by the Wheelwright sisters in Belgium, who tormented her to conform to the latest feminine fashions when she didn't want to. Maybe this is what Emily meant by her retort 'I wish to be as God made me'? She was happy being an unfeminine tomboy of sorts, and didn't want to be femininised by the latest styles just to please someone else. We'll never know, of course, but it's definitely food for thought.

Top Withins, near Haworth. The house does not resemble Emily's Wuthering Heights, but its lonely setting may have provided inspiration.

FEMINIST HEIGHTS

As we've begun to see, *Wuthering Heights* has so much to say about feminism (albeit implicitly, as many see it), but this wasn't always the case, and it wasn't until the 1970s that scholars and critics began to value Emily's feminism thanks to the rise of feminist literary criticism influenced by the second wave of feminism.[15] Original reviewers of the novel found little morality in the text, as one anonymous critic remarked:

> *Wuthering Heights is a strange sort of book, – baffling all regular criticism; yet, it is impossible to begin and not finish it; and quite as impossible to lay it aside afterwards and say nothing about it. In the midst of the reader's perplexity the ideas predominant in his mind concerning this book are likely to be – brutal cruelty, and semi-savage love. What may be the moral which the author wishes the reader to deduce from his work, it is difficult to say; and we refrain from assigning any, because to speak honestly, we have discovered none but mere glimpses of hidden morals or secondary meanings.*[16]

Although the reviewer finds the novel 'strange', they acknowledge ambiguity about its moral 'message', and partly this is because of the love story between Heathcliff and Catherine. Heathcliff, in particular, who hadn't experienced any love in his life before her (as far as we know), loves selflessly, and his grief is beguiling. Yet, it is a deeply dysfunctional form of love and not one that would be readily welcomed (or make for happiness) in the real world. His posthumous love, in particular, is extreme: unearthing his love's grave and taking revenge on everyone who ever slighted him or got in the way of their love. But I don't think their love is as idealistic as we sometimes think; it's only in their final meeting that they interact as lovers and prior to that Catherine had rejected the idea of marrying him and degraded his 'classless' ways. To me, Emily didn't intend this to be a love story to aspire to; in fact, I think the moral message she wanted us to take was one of caution towards idyllic love.

Take Isabella Linton, who is the victim of Heathcliff's scorn and hatred. Although raised in safe and elegant surroundings at Thrushcross Grange, Heathcliff marries her purely to wreak revenge on her brother. In her innocence and naivety, Isabella develops 'a sudden and irresistible attraction towards the tolerated guest', and she was, 'at that time a charming young lady of eighteen; infantile in manners, though possessed of keen wit, keen feelings, and a keen temper, too, if irritated'.[17] Isabella 'pined and fretted' over Heathcliff, we're told, and Catherine tells her – in a rather harsh and blunt manner – not to be guided by her heart:

> 'You are an impertinent little monkey!' exclaimed Mrs. Linton, in surprise. 'But I'll not believe this idiocy! It is impossible that you can covet the admiration of Heathcliff – that you consider him an agreeable person! I hope I have misunderstood you, Isabella?'
>
> 'No, you have not,' said the infatuated girl. 'I love him more than ever you loved Edgar, and he might love me, if you would let him!'
>
> 'I wouldn't be you for a kingdom, then!' Catherine declared, emphatically: and she seemed to speak sincerely. 'Nelly, help me to convince her of her madness. Tell her what Heathcliff is: an unreclaimed creature, without refinement, without cultivation; an arid wilderness of furze and whinstone. I'd as soon put that little canary into

*the park on a winter's day, as recommend you to bestow
your heart on him! It is deplorable ignorance of his character, child, and nothing else, which makes that dream enter
your head. Pray, don't imagine that he conceals depths of
benevolence and affection beneath a stern exterior! He's
not a rough diamond – a pearl-containing oyster of a
rustic: he's a fierce, pitiless, wolfish man. I never say to
him, "Let this or that enemy alone, because it would be
ungenerous or cruel to harm them;" I say, "Let them alone,
because I should hate them to be wronged:" and he'd crush
you like a sparrow's egg, Isabella, if he found you a trouble-
some charge. I know he couldn't love a Linton; and yet he'd
be quite capable of marrying your fortune and expecta-
tions: avarice is growing with him a besetting sin. There's
my picture: and I'm his friend – so much so, that had he
thought seriously to catch you, I should, perhaps, have held
my tongue, and let you fall into his trap.'*[18]

Catherine really couldn't have been any clearer in warning Isabella against allowing – or following – her misguided
infatuation, and in many ways her words are similar to Helen
Huntingdon's aunt, Mrs Maxwell, in *The Tenant of Wildfell Hall*
who, in chapters entitled 'The Warnings of Experience' and
'Further Warnings', cautions Helen against giving her heart
to the caddish rake, Arthur Huntington.[19] Nelly also warns
Isabella against Heathcliff's charm, telling her that he is a 'bird
of bad omen: no mate for you'.[20] And even Heathcliff scorns the
idea that Isabella harbours feelings for him, telling her

*'She wishes to be out of my society now, at any rate!' And
he stared hard at the object of discourse, as one might do at
a strange repulsive animal: a centipede from the Indies, for*

instance, which curiosity leads one to examine in spite of the aversion it raises. The poor thing couldn't bear that; she grew white and red in rapid succession, and, while tears beaded her lashes, bent the strength of her small fingers to loosen the firm clutch of Catherine; and perceiving that as fast as she raised one finger off her arm another closed down, and she could not remove the whole together, she began to make use of her nails; and their sharpness presently ornamented the detainer's with crescents of red[.]

'I'd wrench them off her fingers, if they ever menaced me,' he answered, brutally, when the door had closed after her. 'But what did you mean by teasing the creature in that manner, Cathy? You were not speaking the truth, were you?'

'I assure you I was,' she returned. 'She has been dying for your sake several weeks, and raving about you this morning, and pouring forth a deluge of abuse, because I represented your failings in a plain light, for the purpose of mitigating her adoration. But don't notice it further: I wished to punish her sauciness, that's all. I like her too well, my dear Heathcliff, to let you absolutely seize and devour her up.'

'And I like her too ill to attempt it,' said he, 'except in a very ghoulish fashion. You'd hear of odd things if I lived alone with that mawkish, waxen face: the most ordinary would be painting on its white the colours of the rainbow, and turning the blue eyes black, every day or two: they detestably resemble Linton's.[21]

Here, Heathcliff not only scares and warns Isabella about her affections, but declares with alarming savagery that he would be physically violent towards her should they live alone. And of course, this is exactly what happens: in his plan to seek revenge on Edgar Linton, Heathcliff courts Isabella, elopes with her, and then subjects her to violence and marital abuse.

Some have argued that Isabella is a mere prop in the novel's story to facilitate rivalry and revenge, but this doesn't mean that we should dismiss her story. In fact, Isabella's letter is one of the most overlooked parts of the novel, regularly forgotten amidst the Heathcliff and Catherine love story that forms the first part, and the second generation, which comes after her escape to somewhere in London, where she gives birth to Linton, Heathcliff's son. Of course, what's troubling about Isabella's narrative is that she is effectively punished for falling for Heathcliff. But I think Emily's endeavour can be reframed along the lines offered by Anne in *The Tenant of Wildfell Hall* who, as we've seen, declared her novel a warning to young women and 'rash youths' who might succumb to 'bad' romantic figures.[22] If this is the case, her story is, sadly, relevant today and Emily's novel stands as a feminist commentary on gender and domestic abuse.

SIX

EMILY'S AFTERLIVES

The parsonage and graveyard at Haworth.

Emily died just a year after the publication of her novel. It's tragic that she didn't get to see how her book would be lauded and acclaimed by subsequent generations, nor how much it has influenced modern culture. Since her death, Emily's life and work have been brought to life and transformed repeatedly through various mediums at different moments. And *Wuthering Heights* holds an influential place in literary, filmic and popular culture. Not only has the book been translated into more than thirty languages, but it has inspired frequent adaptations on film, television and stage through to musicals, opera and ballet. With this in mind, this chapter takes a look at some of the ways that Emily's life and work have been reimagined, and it focuses on how 21st-century recreations of the author and her work are reproduced to speak to modern-day concerns. Let's begin by focusing on *Wuthering Heights*.

BEYOND THE HEIGHTS

Emily's literary classic wasn't always so well received, for it stirred controversy on its publication, as we've already seen. As one anonymous reviewer writing in *Graham's Magazine* imaginatively remarked:

> *There is an old saying that those who eat toasted cheese at night will dream of Lucifer. The author of Wuthering Heights has evidently eaten toasted cheese. How a human being could have attempted such a book as the present without committing suicide before he had finished a dozen chapters, is a mystery. It is a compound of vulgar depravity and unnatural horrors.*[1]

Despite this particular reviewer's rather morose concerns,

Wuthering Heights has had a dynamic and enduring legacy. In *Brontë Transformations* (1996), Patsy Stoneman catalogued some of the ways that *Wuthering Heights* and Charlotte's *Jane Eyre* were reworked by almost every generation after the authors' deaths, contextualising the aims and agendas of the reproductions in question. Published in the mid-1990s, Stoneman's book emerged at an important moment, when all things Victorian were once again very much in vogue, especially with the publication – and success of – A.S. Byatt's *Possession* (1990), which won the prestigious Man Booker Prize that year.

By the end of the decade, the genre of neo-Victorianism was firmly established in literary and scholarly circles. Generally, the term 'neo-Victorian' describes materials and objects that engage with, and rework, Victorian literature and/or culture. Often this takes the form of period drama or historical fiction, but it can be more fluid. The BBC's *Sherlock* (2010–), for instance, starring Benedict Cumberbatch, provides a helpful example of the loose nature of the word 'Victorian' in the term. Importantly yet inadvertently, the Brontës have played a significant role in the establishment of the genre, since the publication of Jean Rhys' *Wide Sargasso Sea* (1966), which provides the back story to Bertha Rochester from *Jane Eyre* and is often cited as inaugurating it.

Prequels, sequels, spin-offs and backstories, then, provide one dominant avenue by which contemporary writers and artists engage with the Victorians, and *Wuthering Heights* has inspired plenty of works in this vein. Lin Haire-Sargeant's *Heathcliff: The Return to Wuthering Heights* (1992) is one of the earliest works to fictionalise the blanks in the chronology in Emily's novel, providing an account of the missing three years in Heathcliff's narrative. Following Emily's use of letters in the original, Haire-Sargeant tells the events of Heathcliff's lost period – between the time that he fled the Heights and returned (with a fortune) to Catherine – in a letter that had been delivered on the day of her marriage to Edgar Linton, but which meddling Nelly had hidden from her mistress. Interestingly, Nelly, too, has been given her own voice in Alison Case's *Nelly Dean* (2015), which provides an accompaniment to Emily's novel by retelling the story in more detail solely through Nelly's eyes.

Similar to Haire-Sargeant's novel, Caryl Phillips' *The Lost Child* (2015), also responds to Emily's text, but does so by 'solving' the mystery of Heathcliff's birth. Picking up Emily's themes of origins, orphans and belonging, Phillips makes Heathcliff the illegitimate son of Mr Earnshaw by an African former slave. But there's a twist, for *The Lost Child* combines Heathcliff's tale with a modern-day narrative, focusing on the story of Monica Johnson. Johnson is a promising Oxford student who, in the 1950s, leaves her studies to marry an African-Caribbean graduate. Of course, at this time, there were limited educational avenues open to women, and marriage, especially to an immigrant, places Johnson in a unique situation. Amidst such pressure, their marriage falls apart, but with two children and few options open to her, Monica has little choice but to return home to northern England, where her mental health begins to crumble. The two texts, then, focus on the experience of being outcast and the fight for liberation – and Phillips' novel illustrates how Emily's original continues to address the issues of social isolation and cultural alienation in the present day.

Of all the film adaptations of *Wuthering Heights* that have been produced (of which there are many), Andrea Arnold's hard-hitting *Wuthering Heights* (2011) anticipates Phillips' novel (to some extent) by also speaking to modern-day concerns about race and racism. Arnold's adaptation strips away the period drama sentiment that has often demarcated previous adaptations of the novel and reworks the book's violence within the context of a tale of cross-race passion. As in *The Lost Child*, Heathcliff is affirmed as black; Solomon Glave provides a haunting performance of the quiet, bullied Heathcliff as a child, and James Howson brings to life Heathcliff's intensity as an adult. Both actors speak with British accents, thus leaving open the ambiguity found in Emily's portrayal of Heathcliff in the novel. Heathcliff's vaguely exotic and dark Gypsy image means that he is commonly read as being of African descent, but another possibility from Emily's text is that he is Irish. This may be surprising for some, but during the 19th century, the Irish were subject to the same stereotyping and racial abuse as those of African descent. Whether he is portrayed as black or

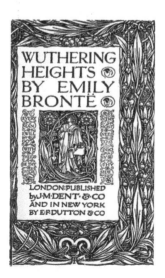

One of many editions of Emily's novel, one of the best-loved works in all of English literature.

Irish, it reminds us of the violence and oppression experienced by immigrant and ethnic minority communities, which of course remains highly relevant today.

Interestingly, in William Wyler's much-loved 1939 adaptation of the novel starring Laurence Olivier and Merle Oberon, Hollywood also used Cathy and Heathcliff's love story as a comment on the racial and cultural boundaries facing the white English and American lovers. But what Arnold's contemporary film shows in more visceral fashion is the physical violence that often accompanies racism when there's a difference in skin colour between partners; something that Emily's book touches on but which, in Arnold's adaptation, is driven home.

The power of Arnold's Heathcliff also comes from the brutality depicted in the scenes that show the physical abuse that Heathcliff endures from Hindley as a child, all of which is explored in the book. Heathcliff is kicked, punched, whipped and abused repeatedly, and Cathy's anger towards her brother's violence is forcefully rendered by her own screams, as well as through the tenderness she bestows on Heathcliff, such as licking his wounds. From this perspective, it's fascinating that early critics of Emily's novel condemned it for lacking an obvious moral message (other than that concerning the destructive nature of obsessive passion), because in modern hands *Wuthering Heights* has never been more amenable to contemporary moral commentary.

In a completely different stance, modern reworkings of *Wuthering Heights* have also – as you'd expect – homed in on the novel's romance. Wyler's 1939 adaptation was among the first to do so, reworking Emily's anti-hero into a tragic romantic figure. Heathcliff (Olivier) and Cathy (Oberon) are either playfully frolicking on the moors or alternately shown in states of saddened contemplation, something poignantly rendered in the famous still image where they sit on the hilltop against a silhouetted sky.

However, in our hyper-sexualised culture, the passion in the couple's romance has been converted into explicit sexual content. I.J. Miller's *Wuthering Nights* (2013) recreates the erotic nature of Catherine and Heathcliff's forbidden passion, and Miller takes quite a few dramatic liberties with Emily's novel (her temerities will no doubt upset as many fans as those who may laugh at it). Heathcliff has sex with just about all the women in the novel in every conceivable manner. Influenced by *Fifty Shades of Grey*, Miller presents Heathcliff as a Victorian Christian Grey: he is a sexual dominant who relishes in the power he has over his submissive lovers and enjoys bringing them to his sex dungeon. A similar bawdy remix can also be found in Annie Cruise's *Fifty Shades of Heathcliff* (2013). This book no longer seems to be available, but suffice to say it takes the events of Lockwood's visit to the Heights and reworks the happenings into an extended sexual orgy.

Beyond these reworkings, MTV has also given us its own interpretation of *Wuthering Heights* (2003). This (embarrassingly bad) musical adaptation transports Emily's brooding Yorkshire romance to a modern-day sunny Californian location. Cate (Catherine) and Hendrix (Hindley) Earnshaw live in a converted lighthouse named Wuthering Heights when (as we know) one day their father beings home an orphan child. Heath, as he's now known, is wildly in love with Cate, but separated from her by the dastardly Hendrix, whose desperately envious of Heath's relationship *and* his musical talents. Amidst such turmoil, Heath pursues a career in rock and he's tattooed and punked up accordingly. Moreover, his tortured love story becomes the inspiration for his music.

So whether you like Heathcliff or not, you can at least enjoy Emily's tale of tragic romance through original songs penned by Jim Steinman, the man behind Meat Loaf's classic album, *Bat Out of Hell* (if you like Heath's style, of course).

EMILY REIMAGINED

It's not only *Wuthering Heights* – Emily herself has been brought to life in fiction and onscreen. But it's important to remember that these sources, in the same way as any regular biography, only present a particular version of Emily, 'selecting and replicating' material to offer their own interpretation of who she was or what she was like.[2]

As mentioned previously, the earliest fictionalisation of Emily lies in Charlotte's second novel, *Shirley*. Charlotte wrote *Shirley* between September 1848 and May 1849, the period when her siblings were dead or dying, and it's after Anne's passing in May that she focused on the novel as an antidote to her grief. Charlotte told Gaskell that Shirley was Emily if Emily had been born to health and prosperity. Consequently, all of Emily's 'rough edges' and quirky personality traits are softened and made palatable to the author and her imagined reader. Shirley Keelder is rich, powerful and 'normal' (whatever that means): she has a happy ending, marries and is welcomed into society. I wonder what Emily would make of herself in this imaginary world?

Beyond the Victorian and into the new millennium, though, Emily's life has continued to be reimagined. Denise Giardinia's *Emily's Ghost* reworks the entirety of Emily's biography and has her as someone that sees ghosts (which is something that plays to the idea that Emily was a visionary and mystic). Giardinia fleshes out some of the gaps and details of Emily's life and also transforms aspects of other Brontë fictions into the novel. For instance, Charlotte's portrayal of Jane Eyre's experience at Lowood becomes Emily's; she's bullied and abused by the Reverend William Carus Wilson, who humiliates her and makes her stand on a stool (like Jane does) for 'telling stories':

> 'Dear Miss Evans. This wretched girl is your charge, I believe. Take her now and stand her on a stool in the schoolroom. Keep in the place for half an hour. And inform the other pupils that for the next week, they are to shun her. Explain to them that their souls will be in danger if they listen to this – this little reprobate and her stories. They should take great care of her.'
>
> 'But – but her sisters,' Miss Evans said, 'her sisters must not shun her? Must they?'
>
> 'They must. They are in more danger than anyone.'[3]

In its combination of sturdy facts and creative fiction, Giardinia's novel also contributes to Brontë mythology, with the sisters' interest in William Weightman amplified. But here the curate also takes a strong interest in the most unconventional Brontë sibling.

In a similar vein, Sarah Fermi's *Emily's Journal* (2006) is an extraordinary and fascinating text. Fermi is a social historian with expert knowledge of Haworth and the Brontës. Despite being a fictitious source, Fermi's text presents itself as authentic. Not only does it recreate an imagined journal by Emily (from childhood), but it provides commentary on the piece by Charlotte and Anne, hence the subtitle 'With annotations by her sisters, Charlotte and Anne' and suggesting that it was 'Edited by Charlotte Brontë', a detail that pays homage to Charlotte's pivotal role in the sisters' literary careers.

The text is built on Fermi's belief that Emily must have had a motive for the passionate love story she created between Catherine and Heathcliff, thus rejecting the idea that it was based on imagination. Accordingly, following her own historical research on the matter, Fermi thus presents a candidate: Robert Clayton. Clayton was born within weeks of Emily's birth. His family were local farmers and weavers and lived locally, but he died aged just eighteen. Fermi surmises that Emily's love for Clayton and her grief at his young death was the inspiration for *Wuthering Heights*, and *Emily's Journal* presents the fictionalised arc for this love story. The result is fascinating because, on the one hand, it is entirely fictitious, but on the other it's based on the author's historical knowledge and detailed research, with circumstantial evidence and supposition thrown in. It's a must-read for any Emily fan craving (imaginary) insight into her inner world.

On-screen approaches to Emily have been somewhat different. One of the earliest known screen adaptations of the lives of the Brontës is *Devotion*, a major Hollywood production from 1946. *Devotion* invests heavily in nostalgia and creative licence coupled with a simplified and romantic take on the sisters. The presence of nostalgia in relation to the Brontës is significant, because as Lucasta Miller notes, 'Often, "Brontë" has come to stand for an all-purpose cosy nostalgia with no connection at all to literature.'[4] Expanding on that, we could say that nostalgia amplifies the tragedy of the Brontë story and adds to the mythology surrounding them but does so in a way that makes it appealing. Curtis Bernhardt's *Devotion* does just this.

Watching *Devotion* today is quite a funny yet cringeworthy experience for any Brontë fan that knows their subject. Other than representing the three sisters as our Victorian Northern heroines, who also wrote novels of the same name, and who interact with characters with names from actual people in the Brontës lives, the film has little historical merit. Writing in the *New York Times* in 1946, Bosley Crowther argued that

> *The Warners have simplified matters to an almost irreducible extreme and have found an explanation for the Brontës in Louisa May Alcott terms. They have visioned sombrous Emily, the author of Wuthering Heights, and Charlotte, the writer of Jane Eyre, as a couple of 'little women' with a gift. Despite an excellent score by Erich Wolfgang Korngold, and production values and an ending that hearkened back to the earlier Wuthering Heights by Warner Brothers' rival studio, the press generally put Devotion down as...a mawkish costume romance, even with identities removed. Presented as the story of the Brontës – and with the secondary characters poorly played – it is a ridiculous tax upon reason and an insult to plain intelligence.*[5]

Crowther's scathing sentiment finds a more succinct corollary in a recent review of the film in *Time Out* magazine, which simply describes it as 'pure hokum'.[6]

So, what's hokum about *Devotion*? Well, it strays widely from reality. Like many of the aforementioned sources, *Devotion* presents the myth that Emily was in love, but presents her love interest as one Arthur Bell Nicholls, Charlotte's real-life husband. Accordingly, the plot revolves around an imagined love rivalry between the sisters, and their tryst gives the title its name, as its tagline indicates: 'It tells ALL about those Brontë sisters!...They didn't dare call it love – they tried to call it Devotion'.

In the film, Nicholls arrives in Haworth and is reasonably interested in Emily, who is played by a studio favourite, Ida Lupino. Her Emily is not a reclusive, shy or stubborn middle sister, but a sensible, thoughtful and self-sacrificing family member. We see the pair spending time together, mainly in the form of walks on the moors, and in one scene she takes Nicholls to an isolated, unnamed property and turns to excitedly divulge to her companion, 'I call it Wuthering Heights!' Naturally, Keeper always accompanies them on their walks, but even he too is transformed and romanticised: no longer is he a huge bullmastiff, but a neatly blow-dried English sheepdog.

Of course, because Emily can't have Arthur, the film provides a substitute love for her in the shape of Branwell, thus fuelling another myth regarding Emily's 'special' relationship with her brother (see Chapter Seven). Their closeness is signalled by the early scene in which she finishes a poem he's reciting, and later she laments to Charlotte over the concerted pressures being placed on him as the only male sibling. This Emily also displays a desperately tender, caring side. We see (in a sanitised 1940s context) Branwell's decline into alcoholism, but Emily doesn't condemn his drinking; she merely conveys her disapproval through solemn glances. And Branwell doesn't die from the ravages of tuberculosis with complications from alcohol and drug abuse; rather, he falls in the rain, and Emily quite literally hauls him out of the gutter where he dies in her arms. Emily's pious self-sacrifice comes about after her brother's death when she realises she wants her sister – who also has eyes for her man – to be happy, and so Emily denies herself love and removes herself from the situation, paving the way for Charlotte's happy nuptials to Nicholls. If only it had happened that way…

My favourite adaptation of Emily, though, is Sally Wainwright's *To Walk Invisible* (2016).[7] This biopic focuses primarily on the latter period of Branwell's life, when his literary and artistic ambitions were beyond reach, and he was in the grips of alcohol and substance abuse. All the hallmarks of Brontë stereotyping and cliché are presented here, but Wainwright reworks them respectfully to portray this often maligned Brontë with dignity and class. For the last part of this chapter, then, I want to explore *To Walk Invisible* a little more because not only is it the most recent Brontë biopic but, I think, the most relevant to 21st-century contexts.

NO LONGER INVISIBLE

Wainwright's biodrama was widely praised as a 'bleak' but 'brilliant' portrayal of the family, and a film that illuminated 'the extraordinary challenges faced by ordinary people'.[8] Indeed, such is the regard with which it has been held that, throughout 2017, props and costumes from the production were integrated into the Brontë Parsonage Museum. The mannequins featuring costumes from the drama were situated around the house museum and became striking stand-ins for Charlotte, Emily and Anne.

Importantly, Wainwright has spoken in detail of how she came to the Brontë story. Not only is she a lifelong fan, but she's committed to telling stories about strong women, usually Northern, as productions like *Happy Valley* (2014–), *Scott and Bailey* (2011–16) and *Last Tango in Halifax* (2012–16) testify. Interestingly, prior to *To Walk Invisible*, Wainwright had been commissioned by the BBC to write a script for a drama based on Sarah Fermi's work (which Fermi herself later reworked as *Emily's Journal*). Ultimately the script wasn't commissioned, but Wainwright went on to adapt the piece for BBC Radio 4. Entitled 'Cold in the Earth, and Fifteen Wild

Decembers' – the name of Emily's poem from 1845 – the play was broadcast in March 2006.

With the conceptual focus on Emily and love of the Brontës in place, Wainwright went on to develop *To Walk Invisible*, steeping herself in Brontë scholarship and describing Juliet Barker's 1995 biography as her 'bible'.[9] She also revisited the sisters' novels and Emily's poetry, commenting that they 'were the things I kept closest to me': 'I find it really hard to talk about poetry but it has a very profound effect on me. I can't imagine anybody being clever enough to write like that. The way that she uses language, the way she chooses words, and to get it down in such a succinct form.'[10]

To Walk Invisible presents Emily as a strong, independent and gutsy Northern woman and really brings out the extraordinary challenge that the sisters encountered in the face of their bleak domestic situation and literary desire to be heard. Chloe Pirrie's portrayal of Emily was wonderful (I get goosebumps every time I watch her), and it's entirely fitting that many critical reviews singled her out for praise. 'Emily, whose uncompromising nature and capacity for absolute fury is captured perfectly by the script and by Chloe Pirrie's performance; neither make her into the freak of legend', remarked Lucy Mangan in *The Guardian*. For me, this statement is hugely important, because as I've argued repeatedly here, Emily is all too often conceived of as either a mysterious mystical force or a genius freak whose shy and reclusive nature is matched by stubbornness, anger and determination. *To Walk Invisible* contextualises these traits far more fairly than has been done before and the effect makes Emily more accessible, understandable and relatable for a modern audience.

Indeed, *To Walk Invisible* respectfully celebrates Emily's character traits, creativity *and* penchant for solitude. In a scene concerning Emily's discovery that Charlotte had invaded her writing bureau, we see a furious Emily challenge her sister. The result is a rather bizarre push on Charlotte's forehead, followed by Charlotte's admission of her wrongdoing. Beyond this, though, once Emily consents to Charlotte's plan, we see her develop as Ellis Bell. It's apt, therefore, that Wainwright's love of Emily's poems finds its way on-screen. We see her recite 'No coward soul' to Anne as they lay on the moors. She tells her sister that she wrote it for her, and while Anne lies back and enjoys her sister's spoken word, a tear of happiness and pride flows gently down her cheek. We also see Emily alone on the moors. In one majestic scene, Pirrie's Emily is shown from a bird's eye view, standing at a cliff's edge overlooking the magnificent Yorkshire landscape. Keeper is by her side and, rightfully, he's a bullmastiff again. There's no sense of sorrow or misery there, just strength, beauty and the oneness of the author in the place she enjoyed the most. In Wainwright's tale of female empowerment, Emily's moments are striking.

Wainwright's commitment to realism is also an important factor in the drama's relevance to the present day. Propelled, I suspect, by 21st-century reality TV culture, the drama refuses the sentiment of traditional period drama and opts instead for a gritty portrayal of Haworth in the mid-19th century. It also captures the challenges facing the sisters as women writers in the period. As I watched the broadcast live in December 2016, I was following social media coverage, too. Twitter erupted in a proverbial feminist fist-pump in the scene where a fiery Charlotte (played by Finn Atkins) challenges her publisher about his doubt that she is Currer Bell, the author of his prized bestseller, *Jane Eyre*: 'What makes you doubt it, Mr Smith?' she defiantly asked. 'My accent? My gender? My size?'[11]

The same grittiness pervades the portrayal of Branwell (played by Adam Nagaitis), whose alcoholism is shown in a more visceral light. In a time when the devastating effects of addiction are no less taboo but more widely spoken of, Branwell's troubled story can, it seems, find a greater place of safety or at least insight. For Emily, this is important because, like *Devotion*, Wainwright also portrays a close bond between Emily and Branwell that emphasises the affection between the siblings as well as the frustrations brought about by Branwell's self-ruinous behaviour. Consequently, there are scenes where the pair poignantly sit howling at the night's sky together alongside moments where Emily helps a drunken and distraught Branwell to bed.

Interestingly, it's through these characters that Wainwright also particularly conveys the strained nature of the Brontës' domestic situation in 1845–46, something achieved through the suggestion of violence (rather than actual violence). On-screen, Emily makes this explicit when she directs Anne to refuse Branwell money should he request it, telling her younger sister that if she does, 'He won't hit you. And if he hits me, I'll hit him back. Harder.'[12] We also see Emily's toughness and temper in a scene where Branwell is departing the parsonage having physically abused his frail father to obtain money. Emily catches up with him and gives him a piece of her mind:

Emily: *Oh, did you get what you wanted? Yeah, you! Are you proud of yourself, eh? Wangling money out of a blind man? A man practically in his seventies.*

Branwell: *Fuck off.*

Emily: *Eh! Come back here and say that. Yeah, go on. Have a go. See what happens.*

Branwell: *I haven't time.*

Emily: *No? Just the blind and the elderly then, is it?*

Branwell: *Otherwise I would.*

Emily: *Course you would!*

Aside from Branwell's profanity here, the scene makes for uncomfortable viewing, especially as Anne and Charlotte stand watching and, in the next scene, we see the injury that Branwell had inflicted on his father. It's important, therefore, that Emily challenges his behaviour. She resists his tyranny by standing up to his violence and challenging his immoral action. Her language is decidedly 21st century ('Yeah, go on. Have a go'), but she defiantly indicates that she will fight back and not tolerate his physical threat ('See what happens'). Pirrie physically punctuates the delivery of these lines with body language that's reminiscent of an episode of *Jeremy Kyle*. Emily squares up to Branwell, something quite unusual in 19th-century period dramas but entirely apt in this story. This in no way sentimentalises violence or glamorises threatening behaviour, but it is, in the context of the Brontë's troubled story, one of the few times that resistance to abuse is shown. Emily stands her ground not just for herself, but for her whole family, thus challenging domestic bullying and condemning abuse.

Recalling Bosley Crowther's scathing words concerning *Devotion*, it seems only right that Wainwright wanted to challenge the idea that the Brontës' lives were akin to those found in a Jane Austen or Louisa May Alcott novel.[13] *To Walk Invisible* carefully dispatches the 'chocolate box' sentiment so often associated with the Brontës.[14] It demythologises them, realises them as the strong, independent women that they were and, importantly, rehabilitates Emily.

SEVEN

EMILY – REAL AND FAKE NEWS

Purporting to be a portrait of Emily created by Charlotte, this 1894 drawing appeared in a magazine. It was immediately denounced as having no likeness of Emily – an early example of 'Emily Fake News'.

In her recent biography of Anne Brontë, Samantha Ellis described her encounter with the vast 'disputatious scholarship' about Emily, recalling how, one day in the parsonage library, she sat feeling as though she could 'hear the biographers all yelling at each other from the battered volumes, a clamour rising and rising, threatening to topple the tall glass-fronted bookshelves and crush anyone foolish enough to try to sift through it all'.[1] Ellis' point is absolutely true and her response is surely one that any Brontë scholar, student or admirer would recognise. It's not just that biographers disagree about the answers to questions that seek to unravel Emily for new audiences, nor that biographers and critics often present conjecture as new knowledge (though this too is an issue in itself). The problem is that, when it comes to Emily, biographers regularly promise to clear up existing confusions about her, but very often they end up creating more.

To end my reappraisal of Emily, then, I want to take up what Ellis describes as a 'foolish challenge', namely, revisit some of the more sensational tales about Emily, both sane and silly, to try and discern which of the stories are real and which ones are misleading and/or simply untrue; fake news, as we call it today. In suitably 21st-century style, I'm presenting this in a list format, but don't let the numbering mislead you – they aren't in any hierarchy; really, the list form is to illustrate just how many myths exist in among the truths. So, let's identify the fake news that circulates about Emily Brontë.

1. EMILY HAD AN UNUSUAL INTIMACY WITH BRANWELL

The idea that Emily had a particularly close relationship with Branwell is a well-trodden path in Brontë biography that's often been used to contextualise the siblings' characters *and* show that Branwell had a heart for someone other than Mrs Robinson (see Chapter One). Some have suggested that the closeness between the middle siblings derived, in part, from the tense relationships that they each had with Charlotte, informing what Lucasta Miller pointedly described as the 'Charlotte-as-bitch' school of thought.[2]

The idea that a brother and sister shared a close relationship shouldn't be surprising, but in the case of the Brontës the closeness has been misconstrued and wildly taken further to suggest that Emily and Branwell had an incestuous relationship, something that's been said of Charlotte and Branwell as well. Naturally, the idea makes for sensational headlines: 'Insanity. Beatings and a brother's forbidden passion,' declared the headline of a *Daily Mail* article from 2011 written by the esteemed author A.N. Wilson.[3]

In Emily's case, the suggestion is based largely on the ropey speculation surrounding the origins of Heathcliff and Catherine. The 'argument' goes that because they were brought up as siblings at the Heights, perhaps their passion was based

Branwell Brontë.

on real-life prototypes, ergo the myth of Emily and Branwell. Even though there is no evidence for this spurious suggestion, it has found its way into modern culture, but at least there it is treated in the manner in which it should be, as this extract from Catherine Lowell's *The Madwoman Upstairs: A light-hearted comedy* (2016) – a neo-Victorian tale based around the Brontës – demonstrates:

> 'So that's it,' I said. 'The greatest love story of all time is an advanced case of incest?'
>
> Orville said, 'Relax, Samantha, it is only a story.'
>
> 'Nothing is ever just a story!' I said. 'Does this mean that Emily Brontë was secretly in love with her brother?'
>
> Orville took a long, exhausted breath. 'Let's not regress, shall we?'[4]

2. BRANWELL BRONTË WAS THE REAL AUTHOR OF WUTHERING HEIGHTS

Here we go, this old chestnut! In 1947, Irene Cooper Willis examined the full history of this allegation, which was made approximately twenty years after the publication of the novel. Her findings remain apt and worth revisiting:

> In a little book which I wrote in 1933, the style of the writing of Wuthering Heights was analyzed and compared with the writing of Branwell's known fragment. It is no exaggeration to say that the writer of the latter could not possibly have written the great novel by 'Ellis Bell'. Branwell's faults of character, admittedly, were made too much of by Mrs. Gaskell and other biographers of Charlotte and Emily; but recognition of this fact and pity for Branwell should

not lead to exaggeration of his literary abilities. The style of Wuthering Heights is the same throughout, intensely dramatic, extraordinarily cogent. There is no cogency whatever in Branwell's story; there are passages of which the reader cannot make head or tail [.]

As to the suggestion made when Wuthering Heights was published, and repeated since, that no woman's hand could have penned Wuthering Heights, that over every page there hangs an 'unmistakable air of masculinity', this hardly requires to be answered nowadays, with the knowledge that we have of the intermixture of so-called male and female qualities in most people.

But virile qualities were noticeable in Emily Brontë. Monsieur Héger said of her: 'She should have been a great navigator.' The truth of his words is proved by her masterly power of steering the story of Wuthering Heights through complex, intricate, and tragic ways to one of the loveliest ends in all English fiction.[5]

Writing some years later, in 1971, Winifred Gérin described Emily's awareness of Branwell's repeated career disappointments and, in 1839, he was preparing for his 'Bradford experiment', his attempts to establish himself as an artist. With little success behind him, Emily, Gérin suggests, helped her brother with his writing:

Her practical good sense (of which she gave constant proof in household matters, in emergencies of illness and acci-dent, even in investing money) told her, however, that Branwell must earn his living, and be encouraged on his way. So she copied his manuscripts for him to leave him free to pursue his painting.[6]

At the very least, Gérin's comment implicitly provides a possibility of there being similarities between the siblings' work. But irrespective of any inadvertent influence, this doesn't amount to the allegations concerned. Suffice to say that Branwell didn't write *Wuthering Heights*, Emily did.

3. EMILY LOVED TO SHOOT

This is true! Emily was indeed a pistol-packing gunslinger (okay, that might be slightly exaggerating it), just like her 'happy' alter ego in Charlotte's *Shirley*. Except it wasn't Emily's own gun, it was her father's. Patrick Brontë had carried a weapon since 1812 and he was, like so many of the English middle class of the 1830s and '40s, alarmed by the civil unrest that was ravaging northern England as workers protested against the new industrial technologies threatening their jobs and livelihoods. Having declared anti-Luddite sentiment in his sermons, Patrick made himself a target for rebellion, so he obtained another weapon and, according to Elizabeth Gaskell, was in the habit of discharging the weapon on a daily basis from a top-floor window in the parsonage. As we've seen, though, we can't always have confidence in Gaskell's biography, but we can verify those aspects of *The Life of Charlotte Brontë* that have been affirmed by other sources. Here, John Greenwood, the Haworth stationer, emerges again, as he documented Emily's gun-toting ways in his journal.

The story goes that as Patrick got older – and because his eyesight was failing (he went to Manchester for cataract surgery in 1846 and the operation was performed without anaesthetic) – he chose Emily over Branwell to shoot and discharge the gun from the parsonage window. In his diary, Greenwood included an extended account of the matter:

Mr Brontë formerly took very great pleasure in shooting – not in the way generally understood by the term, but shooting at a mar, merely for recreation. He had such unbounded confidence in his daughter Emily, knowing, as he did, her unparalleled intrepidity and firmness, that he resolved to learn her to shoot too. They used to practice with pistols [.] his tender and affection 'Now my dear girl, let me see how well you can shoot to-day' was irresistible to her filial nature, and her most winning and musical voice would be heard to ring through the house in response, 'Yes, papa' and away she would run with such a hearty good will taking the board at him, and tripping like a fairy down to the bottom of the garden, putting it in its proper position, then returning to her dear revered parent, take the pistol, which he had previously primed and loaded for her. 'Now my girl' he would say, 'take time, be steady'. 'Yes papa', she would say taking the weapon with as firm a hand, and as steady an eye as any veteran of the camp, and fire. Then she would run to fetch the board for him to see how she had succeeded. And she did get so proficient, that she was rarely far from the mark. His 'how cleverly you have done, my girl', was all she cared for. She knew she had gratified him, and she would go to the kitchen, roll another shelful of teacakes, then wiping her hands, she would return again to the garden, and call out 'I'm ready again, papa', and so they would go on until he thought she had had enough practice for that day. 'Oh!' he would exclaim, 'she is a brave and noble girl. She is my right-hand, nay the very apple of my eye!'.[7]

4. EMILY WAS MUSICAL

Yes, this is true. She played the piano. In fact, Ellen Nussey reported that a piano was added to the parsonage in the mid-1830s and that, 'after some application', Emily 'played with precision and brilliancy'.[8] Her music books reveal that she played Beethoven, Mozart and Haydn. It's likely, therefore, that her love of music is the reason for the appearance of the 'fifteen strong' Gimmerton band in *Wuthering Heights* that, Emily tells us, included 'a trumpet, a trombone, clarinets, bassoons, French horns, and a bass viol, besides singers'. 'They do the rounds of all the respectable houses, and receive contributions every Christmas,' Nelly says, 'and we esteemed it a first-rate treat to hear them.'[9]

5. EMILY WAS A DOMESTIC GODDESS

Well, this might be a bit of an overstatement, but in essence, this is true. In part, this came about when Tabby, the housekeeper, broke her leg and struggled to complete her tasks, so Emily helped out. As a result, she mastered the art of breadmaking, for which her skills became known throughout the town.

6. EMILY WAS WRITING A SECOND BOOK

This is certainly the impression given by a letter that Emily had saved from her publisher, Thomas Cautley Newby, which was found in her writing bureau after she died. The letter was dated 15 February 1848, the year after *Wuthering Heights* was published. It reads:

Dear Sir,

I am much obliged by your kind note & shall have great pleasure in making arrangements for your next novel. I would not hurry its completion, for I think you are quite right not to let it go before the world until well satisfied with it, for much depends on your next work. If it be an improvement on your first novel you will have established yourself as a first-rate novelist, but if it falls short the Critics will be too apt to say that you have expended your talent in your first novel. I shall therefore, have pleasure in accepting it upon the understanding that its completion be at your own time.

Believe me

My dear Sir

Yrs sincerely

T. C Newby [10]

Following her death, however, no evidence of a novel was found, and since then nothing has ever turned up. If she had commenced work on a second novel, we will never know what happened to it. Perhaps, as Barker infers, Charlotte destroyed the incomplete manuscript?[11]

7. EMILY WAS A LESBIAN

Naturally, or so the dubious logic goes, if no identifiable heterosexual lover can be viably identified for Emily, then of course, she must have been a lesbian. The idea that Emily was a lesbian was first suggested by Virginia Moore in *The Life and Eager Death of Emily Brontë* (1936). Moore based her view on biographical and sub-textual readings of Emily's poems, which, she argues, reveal evidence of Sapphic love. Sadly, Moore's credibility was called into question when, in the search for a heterosexual partner for Emily, she misread the title of the poem 'Love's Farewell' as the name 'Louis Parensell', and from that invented a male lover of that name for the author. While Moore's queer reading of Emily's poems fails to convince me *and* willfully conflates gender and sexuality to arrive at the dubious conclusion, it sits amidst a range of readings about the Brontës' same-sex desires.

The esteemed Emily scholar Stevie Davies, for instance, has suggested that her own 'intuition' indicated to her that *Wuthering Heights* 'was not a heterosexual book' and that Emily was a lesbian, but not a practising one, while the lesbian-feminist scholar Sheila Jeffreys published a book that viewed Charlotte's relationship with Ellen Nussey as a homosexual one.[12] There's also been speculation that Charlotte burned Emily's private papers in a homophobic rage in order to censor her sister's queer secret.

I'm not persuaded by the evidence to date. Elsewhere I have written extensively on lesbianism in literature *and* on the importance of valuing queer women writers and the representations of female homosexuality, and I see huge value in asserting the different ways that Emily defied traditional gender and sexual norms. But to go further than that without evidence merely reinforces an outdated and rather heterosexualised notion of lesbianism. The sisters' lives have a lot to say about same-sex bonds, but ultimately, this doesn't amount to homosexuality.

The second part of this fake news story is that Emily had a lesbian relationship with Anne. Not content with the idea that Emily had incestuous relations with Branwell, then, the rumour mill surmises that the closeness between Emily and Anne was also incestuous. I don't think much more needs to be said on this topic. *yawns*

8. EMILY HAD VISITATIONS

Turn-of-the-century writer May Sinclair was the originator of the 'Emily-as-mystic' myth, and subsequent writers have also suggested that Emily, like Lockwood in *Wuthering Heights*, had ghostly visitations. Spirits are part of *Wuthering Heights*' fabric, surfacing everywhere, and from the outset, there is the suggestion that ghosts live side-by-side with the living. Interestingly, in *Jane Eyre*, Helen Burns usefully surmises that 'Besides this earth, and besides the race of men, there is an invisible world and a kingdom of spirits: that world is round us, for it is everywhere...'.[13] Helen's words evoke the haunting scene that closes *Wuthering Heights*: Lockwood returns to the Heights having learned of the doomed, destructive passion of its former tenants when 'an odd thing' happens to him:

> *I was going to the Grange one evening – a dark evening, threatening thunder – and, just at the turn of the Heights, I encountered a little boy with a sheep and two lambs before him; he was crying terribly; and I suppose the lambs were skittish, and would not be guided.*
>
> *'What is the matter, my little man?' I asked.*

> *'There's Heathcliff and a woman yonder, under t'nab,'*
> *he blubbered, 'un' I darnut pass 'em.'*
>
> *I saw nothing; but neither the sheep nor he would go*
> *on so I bid him take the road lower down. He probably*
> *raised the phantoms from thinking, as he traversed the*
> *moors alone, on the nonsense he had heard his parents*
> *and companions repeat. Yet, still, I don't like being out in*
> *the dark now; and I don't like being left by myself in this*
> *grim house: I cannot help it.*[14]

This image is, of course, one that closes the novel. 'The nervous sheep are a fine touch. They know. Baa!' writes John Sutherland.[15] Bizarrely, as I read Sutherland's words, I couldn't help but wonder if the scene had inspired the tormented sheep idea referenced in the classic film *The Silence of the Lambs* (1991), a movie about a serial killer goading a female FBI officer. But come now, that would be creating more myths! Emily, as this quote suggests, clearly enjoyed supernatural tropes, and although she is said to have spent time with her own mother's corpse (another myth?), we will never know whether she was visited by the 'other side'. I'm therefore putting this down as fake news.

9. EMILY WILLED HERSELF TO DEATH

Self-murder, Sutherland reminds us, was Christianity's term for suicide, that most forbidden of Christian sins. This myth has emerged from many distorted readings that have been reworked and refined over the years. As Lucasta Miller describes, Charlotte's addition of a stanza to Emily's poem 'The Visionary' made this Gondal poem appear as if the author was waiting for a power of sorts to 'descend on her from above'.[16]

Moreover, aspects of 'The Prisoner (A Fragment)' (1846), another Gondal poem, have also been taken out of context and interpreted as Emily foreshadowing her own death while challenging herself to 'dare the final bound'.[17]

Certainly, Charlotte wrote that Emily 'made haste to leave us', but this is far more likely a commentary on Emily's early death and refusal of medical help.[18] Nonetheless, Moore's 1936 biography claimed that Emily's 'desire to relive her mystical union with the Absolute led her to commit suicide by self-neglect'.[19] For those wanting more on this subject, Miller's discussion in *The Brontë Myth* handles the topic superbly and guides the reader through the complex heritage of this bizarre myth and how it has gained in currency. For me, though, it's another fake news story.

10. EMILY CAME BACK AS A GHOST

Not only was Emily supposedly susceptible to supernatural visitations but there have been numerous stories citing evidence of Emily's return. Sutherland reports that 'on the lively Ghost Cities' website, an anonymous blogger reported that

> after Emily's death in 1848, she appeared to her last remaining sister Charlotte with her last unpublished work. This so-called 'lost Brontë' is said to be still out there somewhere, perhaps buried in the churchyard at Haworth. Emily's ghost is doomed to wander the moors – much like her heroine Catherine – until this is found and published.[20]

This bizarre story clearly fuels debate regarding Emily's supposed second book. But wonder no more because in October 2014 *Keighley News* reported that Emily had co-written the missing second novel from beyond the grave with the help of a modern-day author. The ghost-writer in question, Morwenna Holman, revealed that Emily had been in communication with her for much of her life and not only published *Westerdale* 'after many hours speaking' with Emily, but had gone on to write a sequel entitled *Heaton*. *Westerdale* is available for purchase via all good retail outlets, and Sutherland, for one, reports that it is an 'interesting read'. Whatever your take on this, attempts to commune and co-write with the literary dead certainly happen, as the controversial collaboration between 'Mark Twain' and Emily Grant Hutchings in the form of *Jap Heron: A novel written via the Ouija Board* (1917) indicates.

11. EMILY WAS A PLAIN JANE

Well, I guess it depends on how you see it. There are only two official portraits of the sisters, both of which were painted by Branwell. There's the 1834 'Pillar' portrait, and there's the 'Gun Group' portrait, from around the same time. The latter was destroyed by Arthur Bell Nicholls, Charlotte's husband, who believed that the family likenesses were poor. However, he tore off part of the painting (destroying the rest), which is believed to be Emily (but many say it is Anne) and that picture – which is known as the 'Profile' portrait – now hangs in the National Portrait Gallery. John Greenwood, the Haworth stationer, who definitely seemed to like Emily, produced a tracing of her image from the 'Gun Group' portrait. The image of Emily in the 'Gun Group' – if it is Emily – is certainly very pretty, serene, even.

While there are a few paintings of Charlotte, when it comes to Emily we only really have Branwell's 'Pillar' portrait and some accounts of her by those who knew her. Emily was very tall with 'kind' eyes that, Ellen Nussey reported, shifted from

These sitters are presumed to be Emily, left; Charlotte, centre;
and Anne, in an 1834 portrait attributed to Landseer.

grey to blue. We also know that she had brown hair and it is
said that she had protruding front teeth. The truth is, though,
that we don't really know what Emily looked like. There are
no photographs or any detailed accounts of her from which
to construct a true likeness. As such, it's impossible to say
whether Emily was a plain Jane or not. It's fitting, though, that
the image of a woman who guarded her privacy so well should
be concealed.

That said, it is worth acknowledging the many images that
are reported to be Emily but which remain disputed. In 2015, a
photograph of three women from the Victorian period found
its way into the press, and speculation as to whether it was the
Brontës was heightened by the fact that an indecipherable word
on the back of the picture was reported to read 'Bells'.[21] Sadly,
this wasn't the first dubious picture of the siblings to surface.
Another, discovered by Lancashire researcher Robert Haley,

was also thought to provide photographic evidence of the sisters. The words '*Les soeurs Brontë, Londres*' (the Brontë sisters, London) was sufficient for the Brontë Parsonage Museum to have the piece analysed. But while experts thought that this was also an image from the period, they believed it was from the 1850s, by which time Emily and Anne were already dead.[22]

Portraiture also throws up some questionable productions. There's the so-called 'Landseer' portrait, by Sir Edwin Landseer (a favourite of Queen Victoria), which came to light in 2011. It is claimed to be of the sisters in 1834, but it remains unauthenticated because the images don't really resemble known likenesses of the sisters.

There's also the illustration of Emily from *The Woman at Home* magazine that is believed to have been painted by John Hunter Thompson around 1840. Written on the back of this image is the caption 'Emily Bronte – Sister of Charlotte B... Currer Bell'. While the scholar Christopher Heywood has critically evaluated the complex history of the portrait, the Brontë Society has its doubts about the authenticity of the piece.[23] Then there's the image pictured on the cover of this book known as the 'Humbert' portrait. Like the other pieces, this has been dated to the 19th century and is captioned 'Emily Jane Brontë'. The signature of the artist is indecipherable, and it has not been validated by the Brontë Society Nonetheless, like the 'Landseer' piece, it was sold at auction and listed as Brontë portraiture.

* ~ * ~ *

So, it is the same with her looks as it is with her personality: there are many different versions of Emily Brontë. Some are true, others are questionable. There are also outright misrepresentations and distortions, and, whatever the provenance of these stories, many of these ideas and images will continue to populate Brontë mythology in the years to come. The life of Emily and her siblings will also breed new speculations and interpretations and give rise to new myths, too.

This book is *my* attempt to navigate some of the material devoted to Emily and shine a light on how I see her 200 years after her birth. How much this would align with the woman herself is something I'll never know. It may not correspond with your own view of who she was.

I'm minded, too, that many may find it a contradiction that, in a book that claims to dispel some of the continued rumours about Emily, an unauthenticated portrait of the author provides the cover image. On the one hand, this criticism is quite true and yet, this in itself reflects the spirit of the book. My own view doesn't always chime readily with existing accounts of her, and as we've seen, those accounts are the source of much debate. Moreover, when I look at Emily's likeness in the 'Pillar' portrait, I see someone who appears physically awkward. I don't really see Emily – or at least, the Emily *I* imagine. That Emily isn't angular, stiff and abstract; she's human.

Interestingly, Edward Chitham provided a slightly modified version of Branwell's portrait on the cover of his biography, suggesting that he too found her likeness wanting somewhat. But even on this revised image, the Emily that stares back at me remains aloof. Stevie Davies once wrote of Emily that she escapes her. I don't feel the same way, and it's the image on the cover of this book – the so-called 'Humbert' portrait – that presents a better likeness of how *I* imagine her: she's more visceral and more real, softer and smiling (ever so slightly).

Giving space to an alternative image of Emily is exactly what I've tried to do in this book. I hope it opens up new ways of thinking about and approaching Emily compassionately and prompts us to think more critically about what we already know about her and how she's portrayed and remembered. And I also hope that the generations of readers who have yet to discover the works of this remarkable Northern woman writer will be as touched by her life and work as I have been.

NOTES & REFERENCES

INTRODUCTION

1   Terry Eagleton, *Myths of Desire: A Marxist Study of the Brontës* [1975] (Basingstoke: Palgrave Macmillan, 2005), p. xxix.
2   No copy of Charlotte's original letter to Southey survives, but we do have his response in which he quotes directly from Charlotte's letter. See Robert Southey to Charlotte Brontë, 12 March 1837, in *The Letters of Charlotte Brontë: With a Selection of Letters from Family and Friends: Volume 1: 1829–1847*, ed. by Margaret Smith (Oxford: Oxford University Press, 1995), p. 166.
3   Lucasta Miller, *The Brontë Myth* (London: Vintage, 2002), p. 170.
4   Emily Brontë, *Wuthering Heights* [1847] (London: Penguin, 1995), p. 3.
5   The portrait is known as the 'Humbert' Portrait and was only discovered in recent years.
6   Charlotte Brontë, 'Biographical Notice of Ellis and Acton Bell', in *Wuthering Heights*, ed. by Pauline Nestor (London: Penguin, 1995), p. xlii.
7   F..R Leavis, *The Great Tradition* (London: Penguin Books, 1948), p. 38.
8   See, for instance, John Sutherland's recent book *The Brontësaurus: An A –Z of Charlotte, Emily and Anne Brontë (and Branwell)*' (2016). While this is a compendium volume about the whole family, Sutherland's 'Preface' begins with his recollection of reading *Wuthering Heights* aged fifteen.
9   Lynn Pykett, *Emily Brontë* (Maryland: Barnes and Noble Books, 1989), pp. 1–2.
10 Samantha Ellis, *Take Courage: Anne Brontë and the Art of Life* (London: Chatto and Windus, 2017), p. 86.

CHAPTER ONE: THE LIFE AND WORKS OF EMILY BRONTË

1   Juliet Barker, *The Brontës* (London: Abacus Books, 1994), p. 110.
2   Patricia Ingham, *The Brontës: Authors in Context* (Oxford: Oxford World Classics, 2006), p. 2.
3   Emily Jane Brontë, *The Complete Poems*, ed. by Janet Gezari (London: Penguin, 1992), p. 125.
4   Admission register of the Clergy Daughters' School, Cowan Bridge, 1824–39, in *The Brontës: A Life in Letters*, ed. by Juliet Barker (London: Viking, 1997), p. 7. A notable error in the school register is the misreporting of Emily's age. She was, in fact, just over six years old at the time of her entry to the school.
5   Charlotte Brontë, *Jane Eyre* [1847], ed. by Stevie Davies (London: Penguin Classics, 2006), p. 7.
6   Elizabeth Gaskell, *The Life of Charlotte Brontë* [1857] (London: Penguin

Classics, 1997), p. 59.

7   Barker, *The Brontës*, p. 110

8   Ingham, *The Brontës: Authors in Context*, p. 5.

9   Barker, *The Brontës,* p. 127.

10 Emily Brontë, 'Untitled Poem – 5', in *Emily Jane Brontë: The Complete Poems*, ed. by Janet Gezari (London: Penguin Classics, 1992), p. 34.

11 Muriel Spark and Derek Stanford, *Emily Brontë: her life and work* (London: Peter Owen, 1960), p. 32).

12 Charlotte Brontë, 'The History of the Year', 12 March 1829, in *The Brontës: A Life in Letters*, ed. by Juliet Barker (London: Viking, 1997), p. 12.

13 *Ibid*, p. 12.

14 *Ibid*, p. 12.

15 Ellen Nussey, 'Reminiscences', in *The Brontës: A Life in Letters*, ed. by Juliet Barker (London: Viking, 1997), p. 25.

16 Juliet Barker, *The Brontës* (London: Abacus Books, 2010), p. 531.

17 Juliet Barker, *The Brontës: A Life in Letters*, ed. by Juliet Barker (London: Viking, 1997), p. 59.

18 Christine Alexander, *The Brontës: Tales of Glass Town, Angria and Gondal* (Oxford: Oxford University Press, 2010), p. 581. Alexander cites from *Esther Alice Chadwick's In the Footsteps of the Brontës* (1914).

19 Gaskell, *The Life of Charlotte Brontë*, p. 104.

20 Emily *Brontë*, *The Complete Poems*, ed. by Janet Gerazi (London: Penguin, 1992), p. 88.

21 Gaskell, *The Life of Charlotte Brontë*, p. 162.

22 Charlotte Brontë to Ellen Nussey, May 1842, *The Brontës: A Life in Letters*, ed. by Juliet Barker (London: Viking, 1997), p. 103.

23 Sue Lonoff, *Charlotte and Emily Brontë: The Belgian Essays* (New Haven and London: Yale University Press, 1996), p. 48.

24 Barker, *The Brontës*, p. 460.

25 Lucasta Miller, *The Brontë Myth* (London: Vintage Books, 2002), p. 197.

26 Charlotte Brontë to Ellen Nussey, 29 October 1848, *The Brontës: A Life in Letters*, ed. by Juliet Barker (London: Viking, 1997), pp. 211–212.

27 Charlotte Brontë to William Smith Williams, 2 November 1848, in *The Brontës: A Life in Letters*, p. 212.

28 Charlotte Brontë to William Smith Williams, 22 November 1848, in *The Brontës: A Life in Letters*, p. 213, and to Ellen Nussey, 10 December 1848, in *The Brontës: A Life in Letters*, p. 215.

29 Barker, *The Brontës*, p. 680.

30 *Ibid*, p. 683.

31 *Ibid*, p. 683.

32 Charlotte Brontë to Ellen Nussey, 23 December 1848, in *The Brontës: A Life in Letters*, p. 218.

33 Charlotte Brontë to William Smith Williams, 25 December 1848, in *The Brontës: A Life in Letters*, p. 219.

34 Charlotte Brontë to William Smith Williams, 4 June 1849, in *The Brontës: A Life in Letters*, p. 237.

CHAPTER TWO: EMILY – THE BIOGRAPHERS' TALES

1   Ellen Nussey, 'Reminiscences of Charlotte Brontë', *Scribner's Monthly* 2:1 (1871), pp. 18–31.

2   Winifred Gérin, *Emily Brontë* (Oxford: Oxford University Press, 1971), p. 36. Emphasis mine.

3   Muriel Spark and Derek Stanford, *Emily Brontë: Her Life and Work* (London: Peter Owen, 1960), p. 16.

4   Elizabeth Gaskell, *The Life of Charlotte Brontë* [1857] (London: Penguin Classics, 1997), p. 111.

5   Charlotte Brontë, 'Biographical Notice of Ellis and Acton Bell', in Emily Brontë, *Wuthering Heights*, ed. by Pauline Nestor (London: Penguin, 1995), p. xxxvi, xxxvii and xiii.

6   *Ibid*, p. xxxvii and xiii.

7   Brontë, 'Biographical Notice', p. xiii.

8   Charlotte Brontë, 'Editor's Preface to the new edition of *Wuthering Heights*' in Emily Brontë, *Wuthering Heights*, ed. by Pauline Nestor (London: Penguin, 1995), p. xiiii.

9   Charlotte Brontë, *Jane Eyre* [1847], ed. by Stevie Davies (London: Penguin, 2006), p. 19.

10   Brontë, 'Biographical Notice', p. xl.

11   Gaskell, *The Life*, p 299.

12   *Ibid*, p. 95 and p. 111.

13   Edward Chitham, *A Life of Emily Brontë* (Oxford: Basil Blackwood, 1987), p. 63.

14   Janis McLarren Caldwell, 'Mental Health', *The Brontës in Context*, ed. by Marianne Thormählen (Cambridge: Cambridge University Press, 2012), pp. 344–351, p. 344.

15   *Ibid*.

16   *Ibid*.

17   Gaskell, *The* Life, p. 104.

18   Lucasta Miller, *The Brontë Myth* (London: Vintage, 2002), p. 172.

19   Juliet Barker, *The Brontës* (London: Abacus Books, 2010), pp. 272–273.

20   Robert Barnard, *Emily Brontë* (Oxford: Oxford University Press, 2000), p. 27.

21   *Ibid*.

22   Emily Brontë, *Wuthering Heights* [1847], ed. by Pauline Nestor (London: Penguin, 1995), p. 124.

23   Dana Stevens, 'Sister Act', *The Washington Post*, 14 March 2004, and Maureen B. Adams, 'Emily Brontë and Dogs: Transformation Within the Human-Dog Bond', *Society and Animals* (2000), 8:2, pp. 169–181, p. 169.

24   Dolores Monet, 'Emily Brontë: Did the Writer of *Wuthering Heights* Have Asperger's Syndrome?', *Letterpile*, 1 August 2017.

25   Katherine Frank, *Emily Brontë: A Chainless Soul* (London: Penguin, 1990), p. 3.

26   *Ibid*, p. 4.

27   *Ibid*, p. 99.

28   *Ibid*, p. 5.

29 Monet, 'Emily Brontë', *Letterpile* (online).
30 Sian Cain, 'Emily Brontë may have had Asperger syndrome, says biographer', *The Guardian*, 29 August 2016.
31 *Ibid.*
32 Alec Brando Mateo, 'Emily Brontë May Have Had Aspergers', *Bookstr*, 31 August 2016.
33 Emily Willingham, 'Did Emily Jane Brontë Have Autism?', *Forbes*, 2 September 2016.
34 *Ibid.*
35 *Ibid.*
36 *Ibid.*
37 Barker, *The Brontës*, p. 463.
38 *Ibid.*
39 Catherine Reef, *The Brontë Sisters: The Brief Lives of Charlotte, Emily and Anne* (Boston, New York: Houghton Mifflin Harcourt, 2012), p. 66.
40 Barker, *The Brontës*, p. 464.
41 Gérin, *Emily Brontë*, p. 34.
42 Lynn Pykett, *Emily Brontë* (Savage, Maryland: Barnes and Noble Books, 1989), p. 15.

CHAPTER THREE: ELLIS BELL

1 Anon, 'From an unsigned review', *Critic*, 4 July 1846, in Miriam Allott (ed.), *The Brontës: The Critical Heritage* (London: Routledge, 1974), pp. 59–60.
2 *Ibid.*
3 Anon, 'From an unsigned notice', *Athenaeum*, 4 July 1846, Allott (ed.), *The Brontës: The Critical Heritage*, p. 61.
4 Algernon Charles Swinburne, from 'Charlotte Brontë: A Note' in Allott (ed.), *The Brontës: The Critical Heritage* pp. 404–412, p. 411; and Peter Bayne, 'On the Brontës', in Allott (ed), *The Brontës: The Critical Heritage*, pp. 324–430, p. 423.
5 Emily Dickinson, 'Letters from Dickinson to Elizabeth Holland', December 1881, EmilyDickinson.org, http://archive.emilydickinson.org/correspondence/holland/l742.html [accessed 10 December 2017]
6 *Ibid*, p. 440.
7 This suggestion is made in Robert Barnard's *Emily Brontë* (2000) and Edward Chitham and Tom Winnifirth (eds), *Selected Brontë Poems* (1985).
8 Juliet Barker, *The Brontës*, pp. 564–565.
9 *Ibid*, p. 565.
10 *Ibid.*
11 *Ibid.*
12 Charlotte Brontë, 'Biographical Notice of Ellis and Acton Bell, 1850' in Emily Brontë, *Wuthering Heights*, ed. by Pauline Nestor (London: Penguin, 1995), pp. xxxvi–xlii, p. xxxvii.
13 Robert Barnard, *Emily Brontë* (Oxford: Oxford University Press, 2000), p. 74.

14   Charlotte Brontë, 'Biographical Notice', p. xxxvii.

15   Margaret Smith (ed.), *The Letters of Charlotte Brontë*, Vol. 2, 1848–1851 (Oxford: Oxford University Press, 2000), p. 752.

16   Emily and Anne Brontë, Diary Paper, 26 June 1837, in *Tales of Glass Town, Angria and Gondal*, ed. by Christine Alexander (Oxford: Oxford University Press, 2010), p. 487.

17   *Ibid.*

18   It's worth noting that Juliet Barker affirms Emily as the author of this piece, but other scholars, such as Fanny Ratchford and Christine Alexander, attribute it to Anne.

19   Emily Brontë, 'Gondal Notes', in *Tales of Glass Town, Angria and Gondal*, ed. by Christine Alexander (Oxford: Oxford University Press, 2010), p. 494.

20   Emily and Anne Brontë, 'Diary Paper', 26 June 1837, in *Tales of Glass Town, Angria and Gondal*, ed. by Christine Alexander (Oxford: Oxford University Press, 2010), p. 490.

21   Emily and Anne Brontë, 'Diary Paper', 30 July 1841, in *Tales of Glass Town, Angria and Gondal*, ed. by Christine Alexander (Oxford: Oxford University Press, 2010), p. 490.

22   *Ibid.*

23   Christine Alexander, 'Introduction', in *Tales of Glass Town, Angria and Gondal*, ed. by Christine Alexander (Oxford: Oxford University Press, 2010), p. xxxvi.

24   *Ibid*, p. xxxvi.

25   Anne Brontë, 'Diary Paper', 31 July 1845, in *Tales of Glass Town, Angria and Gondal*, ed. by Christine Alexander (Oxford: Oxford University Press, 2010), p. 491.

26   Emily Brontë, *The Complete Poems*, ed. by Janet Gerazi (London: Penguin, 1992), p. 99.

27   Fannie Ratchford, *Gondal's Queen: A Novel in Verse* (London: McGraw Hill, 1964), p.41.

28   Emily and Anne Brontë, 'Diary Paper', 26 June 1837, in *Tales of Glass Town, Angria and Gondal*, ed. by Christine Alexander, p. 487.

29   Alexander, 'Introduction', in *Tales of Glass Town, Angria and Gondal*, p. xxxv.

30   Muriel Spark and Derek Stanford, *Emily Brontë: her life and work* (London: Peter Owen, 1960), p. 40.

31   Barker, *The Brontës*, p. 378.

32   Emily Brontë, *Wuthering Heights*, ed. by Pauline Nestor (London: Penguin, 1995), p. 65.

33   Laura Inman, *Poetic World of Emily Brontë: Poems from the Author of Wuthering Heights* (Sussex: Sussex Academic Press, 2014), p. 41.

34   *Ibid.*

35   *Ibid.*

36   Emily Brontë, *The Complete Poems*, pp. 8–9.

37   Inman, *Poetic World*, p. 51.

38   Emily Brontë, *The Complete Poems*, p. 125.

39   *Ibid*, p. 55.

40   Inman, *Poetic World*, p. 45.

41   Emily Brontë, *The Complete Poems*, p. 181.

42   *Ibid*, p. 225.

43   Miller, p. 184.

44   Anonymous, 'From an unsigned review of *Wuthering Heights*', *Britannia*,
       15 January 1848, pp. 223–226, p. 226; Anonymous, *Paterson's Magazine*,
       March 1848, reproduced on *The Reader's Guide to Emily Brontë's
       'Wuthering Heights'* website (see https://www.wuthering-heights.co.uk/wh/
       index)

45   Anonymous, 'From an unsigned review', *Douglas Jerrold's Weekly Newspaper*,
       15 January 1848, in Miriam Allott (ed.), *The Brontës: The Critical Heritage*
       (London: Routledge, 1974), pp. 227.

46   Anonymous, 'From an unsigned review', *Examiner*, January 1848, in Miriam
       Allott (ed.), (London: Routledge, 1974), pp. 220–222, p. 222.

47   G.W. Peck, 'From an unsigned review of *Wuthering Heights*', *American
       Review*, June 1848, in Miriam Allott (ed.), (London: Routledge, 1974), pp.
       235–242, p. 235 and p. 240.

CHAPTER FOUR: EMILY IN NATURE

1   Winifred Gérin, *Emily Brontë* (Oxford: Oxford Unversity Press, 1971), p. 35.

2   *Ibid*, p. 34.

3   Ellen Nussey, 'Reminiscences of Charlotte Brontë', *Brontë Society
       Transactions* 2: 10 (1899), pp. 58–83, p. 76.

4   Edward Chitham, *A Life of Emily Brontë* (Oxford: Blackwell, 1987), p. 80.

5   Clement Shorter, *Charlotte Brontë and Her Circle*, Project Gutenberg eBook,
       p. 179.

6   Virginia Woolf, *The Common Reader: Vol 1* [1925], ed. by Andrew McNellie
       (London: Vintage, 2003), p. 159.

7   Sophie Franklin, *Charlotte Brontë Revisited: A View from the Twenty-First
       Century* (Glasgow: Saraband, 2016), p. 71.

8   Charlotte Brontë to James Taylor, 22 May 1850, *The Brontës: A Life in Letters*,
       ed. by Juliet Barker (London: Viking, 1997), p. 280.

9   Deborah Lutz, *The Brontë Cabinet: Three Lives in Nine Objects* (New York:
       W. W. Norton & Company, 2015), p. 82.

10   Emily Brontë, *Wuthering Heights*, ed. by Pauline Nestor (London: Penguin,
       1995), p. 46.

11   Lutz, *The Brontë Cabinet*, p. 82.

12   *Ibid*, p. 64.

13   Ellen Nussey, 'Reminiscences', p. 76.

14   John Sutherland, *The Brontësaurus: An A–Z of Charlotte, Emily and Anne
       Charlotte Brontë (& Branwell)* (London: Icon Books Ltd, 2016), p. 86.

15   Charlotte Brontë, 'Selections to the Poems of Ellis Bell', *Wuthering Heights*
       [1847], Fourth Norton Critical Edition, ed. by Richard J. Dunn (London

and New York: W. W. Norton and Company, 2003), pp. 318–320, p. 319.

16   *Ibid.*

17   Emily Brontë, *The Complete Poems*, ed. by Janet Gerazi (London: Penguin, 1992), p. 198.

18   Laura Inman, *Poetic World of Emily Brontë: Poems from the Author of Wuthering Heights* (Sussex: Sussex Academic Press, 2014), p. 16.

19   Brontë, *The Complete Poems*, pp. 5–6.

20   Anne Carson, 'The Glass Essay', *Glass and God* (New York: New Directions Books, 1995), pp. 1–38, p. 4.

21   Inman, *Poetic World*, p. 16.

22   Brontë, *The Complete Poems*, p. 91–92.

23   *Ibid*, p. 90.

24   *Ibid.*

25   Brontë, *Wuthering Heights*, p. 4.

26   *Ibid*, p. 336 (footnote 2).

27   See Hilda Marsden, 'The Scenic Background of *Wuthering Heights*', *Brontë Society Transactions*, 13:2 (1957), pp. 111–130.

28   Brontë, *The Complete Poems*, pp. 126–127.

29   *Ibid*, p. 270.

30   Gaskell, *The Life*, p. 199.

31   *Ibid*, p. 199.

32   Shorter, *Charlotte Brontë and Her Circle*, p. 155.

33   Ibid, p. 163.

34   Charlotte Brontë, *Shirley* [1849], ed. by Jessica Cox (London: Penguin, 2006), p. 365.

35   Gaskell, *The Life*, p. 200.

36   *Ibid.*

37   *Ibid.*

38   John Preston, 'The brutal Brontës! Emily beat up her pet dog. Charlotte – plain, toothless and dull – was so spiteful children threw stones at her', 22 October 2015, *The Daily Mail*; Stassa Edwards, 'The animalistic Emily Brontë, and her dog, Keeper', 10 June 2014, *The Toast*.

39   Miller, *The Brontë Myth*, p. 203.

40   *Ibid*, p. 203.

41   Juliet Barker, *The Brontës* (London: Abacus Books, 2010), p. 515.

42   *Ibid*, p. 231.

43   *Ibid*, pp. 230–231.

44   Lutz, *The Brontë Cabinet*, p. 104.

45   *Ibid.*

46   Stevie Davies, *Emily Brontë: Heretic* (London: The Women's Press, 1997), p. 111.

47   *Ibid.*

48   Emily Brontë, '*Le Chat*', in *The Belgian Essays*, ed. and translated by Sue Lonoff (New Haven and London: Yale University Press, 1996), pp. 56–58.

CHAPTER FIVE: EMILY AND FEMINISM

1   Cecil Day Lewis, 'The Poetry of Emily Brontë', *Brontë Society Transactions* 13:2 (1957), pp. 83–99, pp. 94–95.
2   Stevie Davies, *Emily Brontë: Heretic* (London: The Women's Press, 1997), p. 28.
3   Charlotte Brontë, *Jane Eyre* (London: Penguin, [1847] 2006), p. 292.
4   Anne Brontë, 'Preface to the Second Edition', *The Tenant of Wildfell Hall*, ed. by Stevie Davies (London: Penguin, [1848] 1996), p. 3.
5   Héger in Elizabeth Gaskell, *The Life of Charlotte Brontë* [1857] (London: Penguin Classics, 1997), p. 166.
6   Extracts from John Greenwood's diary are reproduced in Winifred Gérin, *Emily Brontë* (Oxford: Oxford University Press, 1971), pp. 146–147, p.146.
7   Ibid, pp, 146–147.
8   Lynn Pykett, *Emily Brontë* (Savage, Maryland: Barnes and Noble Books, 1989), p. 17.
9   Gérin, *Emily Brontë*, p. 21 and p. 23.
10 Lytton Strachey, *Queen Victoria: A Life* [1912] (London: Taurus Parke, 2012), p. 238.
11 Emily Brontë, *The Complete Poems*, ed. by Janet Gezari (London: Penguin, 1992), p. 158.
12 Emily Brontë, *Wuthering Heights*, ed. by Pauline Nestor (London: Penguin, 1995), p. 80.
13 Charlotte Brontë, *Jane Eyre*, p. 517.
14 *Ibid.*
15 As well as the aforementioned work by Sandra Gilbert and Susan Gubar in which they read the novel as a reworking of Milton, there are a number of feminist readings of Emily's work; too many, in fact, to name them all here, but there are some canonical pieces to point out. Carol Ohmann's influential paper 'Emily Brontë in the Hands of Male Critics', for instance, drew attention to the various biases of Victorian reviewers and the patriarchal and sexist manner of modern commentators (1971), and Stevie Davies has picked up Gilbert and Gubar's thread to read Brontë as a literary descendent of Milton more widely in her 1988 book. Margaret Homans, meanwhile, has used psychoanalysis to read Emily's poetry (1980), and more recently Judith Pike has written on marriages and the laws of coveture in *Wuthering Heights* (2009).
16 Anonymous, 'Review of *Wuthering Heights*', *Douglas Jerrod's Weekly Newspaper*, 15 January 1848, *The Reader's Guide to Wuthering Heights* online.
17 Brontë, *Wuthering Heights*, p. 100.
18 *Ibid*, pp. 101–102.
19 Anne Brontë, *The Tenant of Wildfell Hall* [1848], ed. by Stevie Davies (London: Penguin, 1996).
20 Brontë, *Wuthering Heights*, p. 102.
21 *Ibid*, p. 105.
22 Brontë, 'Preface to the Second Edition', p. 3.

CHAPTER SIX: EMILY'S AFTERLIVES

1   'Unsigned notice of *Wuthering Heights*', *Graham's Magazine*, July 1848, reproduced in Miriam Allott (ed.), *The Critical Heritage* (London and New York: Routledge, 1974), pp. 242–243.
2   Amber Regis, 'Charlotte Brontë on stage: 1930s biodrama and the archive/museum performed' in Amber Regis and Deborah Wynne (eds.), *Charlotte Brontë: Legacies and Afterlives* (Manchester: Manchester University Press, 2017), pp. 116–141, p. 118.
3   Denise Giardinia, *Emily's Ghost* (London and New York: W.W. Norton & Company, 2009), pp. 29–30.
4   Lucasta Miller, *The Brontë Myth* (London: Vintage, 2002), p. 107.
5   Bosley Crowther, The Screen: 'Devotion', A Fictionalized Tale of Brontë Sisters', *The New York Times*, 6 April 1946.
6   GA, 'Review: Devotion', *Time Out*, n.d.
7   Other important biopics include the BBC's *The Brontës of Haworth*, a six-piece drama from the 1970s that's quite dated now, but nonetheless astute in its detail, and Polly Teale's play *Brontë* (2005). A detailed discussion of Brontë afterlives can also be found in Amber Regis and Deborah Wynne's collection, *Charlotte Brontë: Legacies and Afterlives* (2017).
8   Lucy Mangan, '*To Walk Invisible* review – a bleak and brilliant portrayal of the Brontë family', *The Guardian*, 30 December 2016.
9   Sally Wainwright quoted in Gerard Gilbert, 'The TV drama of the season: *To Walk Invisible*', *The Independent*, 27 December 2016.
10 Sally Wainwright, '*To Walk Invisible*: Interview with Sally Wainwright', *Open Learn*, 9 December 2016.
11 Sally Wainwright, *To Walk Invisible*, BBC and Masterpiece, 2016.
12 *Ibid.*
13 Wainwright in Gilbert, 'The TV drama of the season', *The Independent*.
14 *Ibid.*

CHAPTER SEVEN: EMILY – REAL AND FAKE NEWS

1   Samantha Ellis, *Take Courage: Anne Brontë and the Art of Life* (London: Chatto and Windus, 2017), p. 86.
2   Lucasta Miller, *The Brontë Myth* (London: Vintage, 2002), p. 137.
3   See A.N. Wilson, 'Insanity. Beatings and a brother's forbidden passion. As a lost book by Charlotte Brontë is auctioned, the truth about literature's oddest family', *Daily Mail*, 12 November 2011.
4   Catherine Lowell, *The Madwoman Upstairs: A light-hearted literary comedy* (London: Quercus Editions Ltd, 2016), loc. 2438 of 5071.
5   Irene Cooper Wilson, 'The Authorship of *Wuthering Heights*', *The Trollopian* 2:3 (1947), pp. 157–168, p. 168–169.
6   Winifred Gérin, *Emily Brontë* (Oxford: Oxford University Press, 1971), p. 97.
7   John Greenwood quoted in Gérin, *Emily Brontë*, pp. 147–148.

8   Ellen Nussey, 'Reminiscences of Charlotte Brontë', *Brontë Society Transactions* 2: 10 (1899), pp. 58–83, p. 79.

9   Emily Brontë, *Wuthering Heights* [1847], ed. by Pauline Nestor (London: Penguin, 1995), p. 59.

10   Thomas Cautley Newby to 'Ellis Bell', 15 February 1848, *The Brontës: A Life in Letters*, ed. Juliet Barker (London: Viking, 1997), p. 183.

11   See Juliet Barker, *The Brontës* (London: Abacus Books, 2010), p. 579.

12   Stevie Davies, *Emily Brontë: Heretic* (London: The Women's Press, 1997), p. 199.

13   Charlotte Brontë, *Jane Eyre* [1847] (London: Penguin, 2006), p. 83.

14   Brontë, *Wuthering Heights*, p. 333–334.

15   John Sutherland, *The Brontësaurus: An A–Z of Charlotte, Emily and Anne Brontë (& Branwell)* (London: Icon Books Ltd, 2016), p. 55.

16   Miller, *The Brontë Myth*, p. 226.

17   *Ibid.*

18   *Ibid.*

19   *Ibid.*

20   Sutherland, *The Brontësaurus*, p. 144.

21   A copy of the photograph in question was reproduced in *The Guardian*, 20 July 2015: https://www.theguardian.com/news/shortcuts/2015/jul/20/photograph-of-bronte-sisters

22   A copy of Robert Haley's photograph can be found on the Brontë Parsonage website: http://www.bronte.org.uk/whats-on/news/9/is-this-a-photo-of-the-bronte-sisters-together

23   See Christopher Heywood, 'Found: The "Lost" Portrait of Emily Brontë', *Brontë Studies* 40:2, pp. 85–103.

SELECTED BIBLIOGRAPHY

Christine Alexander, *The Brontës: Tales of Glass Town, Angria and Gondal* (Oxford: Oxford University Press, 2010)

Miriam Allott (ed.), *The Brontës: The Critical Heritage* (London: Routledge, 1974)

Juliet Barker, *The Brontës* (London: Abacus Books, 1994)

Robert Barnard, *Emily Brontë* (Oxford: Oxford University Press, 2000)

Edward Chitham, *A Life of Emily Brontë* (Oxford: Basil Blackwood, 1987)

Katherine Frank, *Emily Brontë: A Chainless Soul* (London: Penguin, 1990)

Elizabeth Gaskell, *The Life of Charlotte Brontë* [1857] (London: Penguin Classics, 1997)

Winifred Gérin, *Emily Brontë* (Oxford: Oxford University Press, 1971)

John Hewish, *Emily Brontë: A Critical and Biographical Study* (Basingstoke: Palgrave Macmillan, 1969)

Patricia Ingham, *The Brontës: Authors in Context* (Oxford: Oxford World Classics, 2006)

Laura Inman, *Poetic World of Emily Brontë: Poems from the Author of Wuthering Heights* (Sussex: Sussex Academic Press, 2014)

Sue Lonoff, *Charlotte and Emily Brontë: The Belgian Essays* (New Haven and London: Yale University Press, 1996)

Lucasta Miller, *The Brontë Myth* (London: Vintage Books, 2002)

Lynn Pykett, *Emily Brontë* (Savage, Maryland: Barnes and Noble Books, 1989)

INDEX

Aeneid (Virgil) 28

alcohol addiction (Branwell) 31, 114, 144–45, 148

Angria 23–24, 35, 70–71, 74, 90

anorexia 54–58

Ars Poetica (Horace) 28

Asperger's syndrome 54, 57–58

autism 57–58

Aykroyd, Tabitha ('Tabby') 4, 26, 35, 86–87, 108–9, 158

Barker, Juliet 18, 47, 76, 146, 159

Bewick, Thomas 28: *History of British Birds, A* 28

Blackwood's Magazine 21

bog burst (1824) 19, 116

Bolton Abbey 36

Bradford 14, 155

Bradley, John 35

Branwell, Elizabeth ('Aunt Branwell') 15, 20, 21, 30, 35, 36, 56

Bridlington 36

Brontë Myth, The: see Miller, Lucasta

Brontë, Anne ('Acton Bell') 4, 9, 14, 17, 19, 20, 22–24, 25–26, 30, 34, 35, 36, 37, 43, 45, 46, 61, 66–67, 68–69, 70, 71, 76, 94, 108, 111, 115, 118, 119, 123, 131, 140, 141, 145, 148–49, 152, 161, 164, 166: *Agnes Grey* 30, 37, 82, 115; death 34, 37, 140; *Tenant of Wildfell Hall, The* 37, 45, 118–19, 129, 131

Brontë, Branwell 3, 4, 14, 17, 19, 22–24, 25, 31, 34, 35, 37, 47–48, 91, 94, 144–45, 148–49, 152–56, 161, 164, 167: addiction 31, 114, 144–45, 148; death 31, 34, 37, 144; *History of the Young Men, The* 47;

portraits and other art 3, 4, 39, 63, 164, 167

Brontë, Charlotte ('Currer Bell') 3–5, 6, 7, 11, 14, 16–17, 20, 22–24, 24–26, 27–30, 31–32, 34, 35, 36, 37, 40, 41–48, 50–56, 59–60, 61, 65–68, 69, 76, 82–84, 90–92, 95, 108, 109, 111, 112, 118–19, 120, 126, 140–42, 143, 144, 145, 147, 149, 153, 154, 156, 159, 160, 162–63, 164, 166: *Jane Eyre* 3, 6, 16, 28, 37, 44, 84, 118, 125, 135, 141, 143, 147, 161; *Professor, The* 37; *Shirley* 11, 37, 42, 108, 112, 120–21, 140, 15; *Villette* 37

Brontë, Elizabeth 14, 16, 17, 35: death 16, 35

Brontë, Emily: biographers' interpretations of 39–62 *see also individual authors and scholars*; childhood 14–23; death 32–34, 37, 69, 82, 134, 135, 159; faith 7–8, 18, 20; fantasy and supernatural 11, 21, 23, 26, 55, 70–71, 123, 162, 163–64; feminism 8, 10, 117–32; fictionalisation of in *Shirley* 11, 37, 42, 108, 112, 120–21, 140, 156; mental health of 41, 49–58, 136; myths about 5, 12, 41–48, 94, 110, 141–44, 151–68; nature, influence of 11, 19, 72, 90–116; poetry 7–8, 15, 19–20, 21, 24, 27–28, 30, 36, 37, 42, 64, 65–69, 82–83, 91, 95–96, 96–98, 99–101, 101–3, 104–5, 124, 146, 147, 160, 162, 163; portraits of *see separate entry*; shyness 9, 31, 40–41, 45–46, 54–55, 90, 95, 144, 146; teaching

27–28, 59–60; *Wuthering Heights see separate entry*
Brontë, Maria (Emily's mother) 14, 35
Brontë, Maria (Emily's sister) 14, 15, 16, 17, 35: death 16, 35
Brontë Parsonage Museum, the 2, 93, 107, 108, 145, 166
Brontë, Patrick 14, 15–19, 20, 22, 28, 32, 35, 37, 40, 49, 57, 76, 90, 94, 148–49, 156
Brontë Society, the 118, 166
Brontë Studies 118
Brontës, The: see Barker, Juliet
Brussels 29, 36, 76
Bush, Kate 2
Byron, Lord George Gordon 21, 73, 91
Caldwell, McLarren 49
'*Chat, Le*' 29, 112–13, 115
Chitham, Edward 47–48, 167
Clergy Daughters' School, Cowan Bridge 15–16, 20, 35, 51
Coleridge, Samuel Taylor 91
Cowan Bridge 16, 20, 35, 51
Davies, Stevie 119, 160, 167
Day Lewis, Cecil 118
Diary Papers, the 4, 24–26, 66, 71, 86, 106, 108
Eagleton, Terry 3
Evans, Anne 16
Evans, Mary Ann (George Eliot) 68
feminism 6, 8, 10, 11, 55, 117–32, 147, 160
Fermi, Sarah 141–42, 145
Frank, Katherine 55
Franklin, Sophie 92
Garrs, Nancy and Sarah 15, 19
Gaskell, Elizabeth 5, 17, 18, 29, 37, 42, 45–46, 47, 48, 50, 54, 57, 58, 61, 75, 106, 108–11, 112, 140, 154, 156: *Life of Charlotte Brontë, The* 5, 17, 37, 42, 45–46, 109–10, 156
Gérin, Winifred 61, 123, 155–56
Giardina, Denise 17

Glass Town 23–24, 35, 74
Gondal 11, 24, 25–26, 30, 35, 36, 58–63, 65–67, 69–74, 75, 77, 81, 82, 83, 123, 124, 162, 163
Greenwood, John 122, 156, 164
Haley, Robert 165–66
Halifax 27, 36, 89, 104, 105,
Harman, Claire 57–58
Haworth 14, 16, 17, 32, 35, 36, 51, 75, 93, 94, 99, 106, 122, 141, 144, 147, 163
Haworth Parsonage 2, 3, 4, 14, 35, 93, 107, 108, 133, 145, 166
Héger, M. Constantin 29, 61, 62, 76, 113, 120, 155
Hewish, John 48, 52
High Sunderland 89, 104
incest 153–54, 161
Inman, Laura 77
Keeper (Emily's dog) 4, 32, 59, 107–11, 115–16, 122, 144, 147
Law Hill school (Miss Patchett's) 27, 36, 104
Leavis, FR 6, 16, 79
lesbianism 160–61
Life of Charlotte Brontë, The: see Gaskell, Elizabeth
Marsden, Hilda 104
Miller, IJ 139
Miller, Lucasta 12, 47, 50, 110–11, 142, 153, 16, 163: *Brontë Myth, The* 47, 50, 110–11, 163
Nero (Emily's merlin) 106–7
Newby, Thomas Cautley 37, 158–59
Nicholls, Arthur Bell 37, 143–44, 164
Nussey, Ellen 24, 29, 31, 32, 35, 36, 40, 46, 61, 62, 90, 94, 158, 160, 164
opium 31
Parry, Sir William Edward 22–23
Pensionnat Héger 36, 59, 61
Phillips, Caryl 136–37
Poems by Currer, Ellis and Acton Bell 37, 64
portraits of Emily Brontë (real and

disputed) 3, 63, 151, 165–66: Branwell's 63; 'Gun Group' portrait 164; Getty 13; Humbert ii, 5, 167–68; Landseer 165, 166 'Pillar' portrait 3, 4–5, 164, 167; 'Profile' portrait 63; Richmond 3

Pykett, Lynn 119, 122

Richmond, George 3

Roe Head 20, 35, 50, 52

Romantics, the 21, 91 *see also individual writers and artists*

Scarborough 37

Scribner's Monthly 40

Shorter, Clement King 40, 107

Southey, Robert 3, 65, 91

Spark, Muriel 75

Taylor, Joseph 29

Taylor, Mary 29, 35

Ponden Hall 86

To Walk Invisible 144–45, 146–47, 149

Top Withins (Withens) 94

toy soldiers 22–24, 35

tuberculosis 16, 31, 35, 144

Verdopolis 23

Victoria, Queen 123–24, 166

Wainwright, Sally 144–45, 146–49

Weightman, William 76, 141

Williams, William Smith 33, 34

Willingham, Emily 57–58

Wooler, Miss (school at Roe Head) 20, 35, 50, 52

Wordsworth, William 21, 91

Wuthering Heights 2, 3, 4, 5, 6, 11, 26, 30, 37, 41, 43–45, 46, 52, 54, 64, 71, 77, 79, 82, 84–87, 93–94, 103, 104, 111, 119, 124, 125, 127–31, 134–40, 142, 143, 144, 154–56, 158, 160, 161–62: Catherine Earnshaw 44, 52, 77, 79, 124–25, 127–31; Cathy Linton 2, 77, 93–94, 125–26, 130, 138; Heathcliff 4, 6, 44–45, 52–53, 77, 79, 86, 93, 94, 125–26, 127, 128–31, 135–39, 142, 153; Lockwood 4, 46, 86, 93, 103, 139, 161; Nelly Dean 86, 125; Thrushcross Grange 4, 53, 86, 128

York 26, 36

ACKNOWLEDGEMENTS

I'm very grateful to Sara and Craig at Saraband for their enthusiasm and support for this project, and their kindness and encouragement to me throughout its duration. I'm also thankful to all the students I had the pleasure of teaching on my Brontës module while at Brunel University, London, where many wonderful discussions and debates were had about all things Brontë, as well as a bit of Heathcliff-mania at times. Finally, I have a huge debt of thanks to Sophie Franklin for being such a wonderful collaborator and an inspiration; her companion volume on Charlotte was enormous fun and opened up a space for me to be a nerdy scholar and Brontë fan at the same time.

ABOUT THE AUTHOR

Dr Claire O'Callaghan is a Lecturer in English in the School of Arts, English and Drama at Loughborough University, where her research focuses on Victorian and neo-Victorian literature and culture, with an emphasis on gender, sexuality and queerness. She has published widely on these topics.

CHARLOTTE BRONTË REVISITED

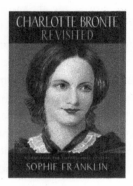

DISCOVER THE REAL CHARLOTTE BRONTË

World-famous for her novel *Jane Eyre*, Charlotte Brontë is a giant of literature and has been written about in reverential tones in scores of textbooks over the years. But what do we really know about Charlotte?

Sophie Franklin offers a fresh, original and entertaining take on Charlotte and her works. She reveals Charlotte's private world of convention, rebellion and imagination, and how these features shaped her life, writing and obsessions – including the paranormal, nature, feminism and politics.

Also including a guide to the best Brontë places to visit in the UK and beyond, this is a celebration of all things Charlotte, and emphatically shows why she's as relevant today as she ever was.